THE ESSENTIAL CARDINAL NEWMAN COLLECTION

"In the case of Newman, one is dealing not simply with a theological but with a spiritual master, one who laid out the dimensions of Christian life—its basic presumptions and practices—and who uncovered obstacles to Christian living."

From the afterword by Cyril O'Regan,
Ratzinger Prize laureate
Huisking Professor of Theology at the University of Notre Dame

"This careful arrangement of texts and translations by Newman contains many inspiring reflections and prayers. Maintaining an intimate tone while steeped in scripture and doctrine, these reflections and prayers praise God's beauty and providence and take us into Christ's suffering and Real Presence."

Fr. Juan R. Vélez
Editor of *A Guide to John Henry Newman: His Life and Thought*

"He is worthy to take his place in a long line of saints and scholars. In St. John Henry, that tradition of gentle scholarship, deep human wisdom, and profound love for the Lord has borne rich fruit, as a sign of the abiding presence of the Holy Spirit deep within the heart of God's people, bringing forth abundant gifts of holiness."

Pope Benedict XVI

"Newman's spiritual writings unveil the joyful simplicity at the heart of the Gospel: to love and to be loved. What a remarkable thing it is to pray both with and to Newman, to join our voices with his, to make his words gathered here in this volume somehow our own."

From the foreword by Jennifer Newsome Martin
Associate professor at the University of Notre Dame and
Director of the de Nicola Center for Ethics and Culture

THE ESSENTIAL CARDINAL NEWMAN COLLECTION

*Prayers, Meditations, and
Other Spiritual Writings*

JOHN HENRY NEWMAN

Christian Classics ⳥ *Notre Dame, Indiana*

Cum Permissu Superiorum
Nihil Obstat: Arthur J. Scanlan
Censor Librorum
Imprimatur: Patrick Cardinal Hayes
Archbishop of New York

The *Nihil Obstat* and *Imprimatur* are official declarations that a book or pamphlet is free of doctrinal or moral error. No implication is contained therein that those who have granted the *Nihil Obstat* or *Imprimatur* agree with its contents, opinions, or statements expressed.

First published 1938 by America Press as *Heart to Heart: A Cardinal Newman Prayerbook,* compiled from his writings by Daniel M. O'Connell, SJ.

Foreword © 2025 by Jennifer Newsome Martin

Afterword © 2011 by Cyril O'Regan

Founded in 1865, Ave Maria Press is a ministry of the United States Province of Holy Cross.

www.avemariapress.com/christian-classics

Paperback: ISBN-13 978-0-87061-326-5

E-book: ISBN-13 978-0-87061-327-2

Cover images © Getty Images.
Cover design by Brianna Dombo.
Text design by Esther Moody.

Printed and bound in the United States of America.

Library of Congress Cataloging-in-Publication Data is available.

CONTENTS

FOREWORD

John Henry Newman (1801–1890) is a figure in the Catholic intellectual tradition perhaps best known for his contributions to theories of the development of doctrine, holistic liberal education, the laity, conscience, and the nature of human reason and belief, as well as his dramatic public conversion from Anglicanism to Catholicism in 1845 and profound influence on Catholic luminaries such as Gerard Manley Hopkins; G. K. Chesterton; Yves Congar, OP; and Pope Benedict XVI. His extraordinary facility with multiple genres of writing—philosophical, juridical, poetical, fictional, rhetorical, homiletic, apologetic, and spiritual—invites appreciation not only for his theological genius but also for his literary genius: James Joyce's *A Portrait of the Artist as a Young Man* has Stephen Dedalus recall the superlative "cloistral silverveined prose of Newman" and make the admission that "many say that Newman has the best prose style"!

However, St. John Henry Newman, canonized in 2019, is not simply a theological and literary genius; he is also a *spiritual* genius, even as he likely would have felt a bit sheepish for being called such. The great beauty of his spirituality is not only the tenderness, intimacy, and affection with which he addresses God but also the depths of his own self-knowledge as one radically transformed and sanctified by grace. Without compromising one jot or tittle on the sophistication of his theological reflections on the Holy Trinity, Christ, Our Lady, the saints, or any other theological loci, Newman's spiritual writings unveil the joyful simplicity at the heart of the Gospel: to love and to be loved.

To receive this love and to return it to God in prayer and worship need not be a spectacle. Newman thinks, rather, of the quiet drama of communing with God as something more akin to Elijah's "still, small voice" spoken into the most intimate and sacred interior depths of the self, in and as what Newman calls the "most innermost heart": "I recognize Thy voice in my own intimate consciousness," he writes. "I turn round and say *Rabboni*." This theme of intimate hiddenness runs like a golden thread throughout Newman's corpus: God is "hidden" within the soul; Christ once "hidden" within the womb of Mary; the kingdom of God "hidden" within the visible world; the "hidden" life and powers of springtime bursting forth in the created order. Even the personal and utterly singular mission of one's own life might be hidden from us this side of heaven. Newman assures his readers, however, that "God has created me to do Him some definite service; He has committed some work to me which He has not committed to another. I have my mission—I never may know it in this life, but I shall be told it in the next. Somehow I am necessary for His purposes." As Jesus hiddenly accompanies the spiritual pilgrim as an "elder brother" upon whose steady presence I can "repose my whole heart on one so gentle, so tender, so familiar, so unpretending, so modest, so natural, so humble," Newman too offers himself as a calm, compassionate, but firm spiritual counselor along the journey, voicing by turns encouragement and consolation.

To come to know Newman is also to come to know his friends: St. Joseph the Worker; the Blessed Mother; St. Paul the Apostle; St. Augustine and his mother, St. Monica; St. Philip Neri. In an unfinished novena to his patron saint, Philip Neri, Newman wrote, "I put myself into thy hands, and for the love of Jesus, for that love's sake which chose thee and made thee a saint, I implore thee to pray for me." As he put himself into the hands of St. Philip Neri, may readers of this collection likewise entrust themselves into the hands of St. John Henry Newman, which are entwined with and held up by such a great cloud of witnesses. To make such an act of surrender, of course—to rest in the economy of the giftedness of communal prayer and intercession—is to admit our own incapacity to go it alone and thus to dispose ourselves entirely into the hands of God.

This curated collection of prayers, meditations, and spiritual writings was originally compiled in 1938 by Daniel M. O'Connell, SJ, long before Newman was declared a saint. Uncluttered by in-text citations or cumbersome footnotes, the texts flow lightly from grace to grace, from gift to gift, inducting the contemporary reader not only into Newman's agile mind but also into the capacious interior of his luminously gentle, humble heart. A lifetime of attentive spiritual and biblical reading, deep prayer, friendship with God and with the Mother of God, and fidelity to the truth and to the Church in equal measure both formed and transformed Newman's spiritual life and imagination. Even as his doctrine is eminent, his argumentation incontrovertibly clear, his intellect rigorous, and his prose style delightfully rich, it is the integrity and the beauty of Newman's inner life that ultimately compels us to a life of prayer. *Cor ad cor loquitur*: "Heart speaks to heart." What a remarkable thing it is to pray both with and to Newman, to join our voices with his, to make his words gathered here in this volume somehow our own.

Jennifer Newsome Martin

John J. Cavanaugh Associate Professor of the Humanities

Department of Theology and Program of Liberal Studies

University of Notre Dame

— I. —
HOLY TRINITY

It is a want in my nature to have one who
can weep with me, and rejoice with me,
and in a way minister to me; would this
be presumption in me, and worse, to hope
to find in the Infinite and Eternal God?

IN THE NAME OF GOD

In the name of God
The Omnipotent Father, who created thee!
. . . in the name of Jesus Christ, our Lord,
Son of the living God, who bled for thee!
. . . in the name of the Holy Spirit, who
Hath been poured out on thee! . . . in the name
Of Angels and Archangels; in the name
Of Thrones and Dominations; in the name
Of Princedoms and of Powers; and in the name
Of Cherubim and Seraphim, . . .
. . . in the name of Patriarchs and Prophets;
And of Apostles and Evangelists,
Of Martyrs and Confessors; in the name
Of Holy Monks and Hermits; in the name
Of Holy Virgins; and all saints of God,
Both men and women, . . .
And may thy place today be found in peace,
And may thy dwelling be the Holy Mount
Of Sion:—through the Same, through Christ, our
        Lord.

Contemplate then the Supreme Being, the Being of beings. . . . He is one; He has no rival; He has no equal; He is unlike anything else; He is sovereign; He can do what he will. He is unchangeable from first to last; He is all-perfect; He is infinite in His power and in His wisdom, or He could not have made this immense world which we see by day and night. Amen.

MAGNAE DEUS POTENTIAE

O God, who hast given
    the sea and the sky,
To fish and to bird
    for a dwelling to keep,
Both sons of the waters,
    one low and one high,
Ambitious of heaven,
    yet sunk in the deep;
Save, Lord, Thy servants,
    whom Thou hast new made
In a laver of blood,
    lest they trespass and die;
Lest pride should elate,
    or the flesh should degrade,
And they stumble on earth,
    or be dizzied on high.
To the Father and Son
And the Spirit be done,
Now and always
Glory and praise.

AETERNA COELI GLORIA

Glory of the eternal Heaven,
Blessed Hope to mortals given,
Of the Almighty Only Son,
And the Virgin's Holy One;
Raise us, Lord, and we shall rise
    In a sober mood,

And a zeal, which glorifies
    Thee from gratitude.
Now the day-star, keenly glancing,
Tells us of the Sun's advancing;
While the unhealthy shades decline,
Rise within us, Light Divine!
Rise, and risen, go not hence,
    Stay, and make us bright,
Streaming through each cleansed sense,
    On the outward night.
Then the root of faith shall spread
In the heart new fashionèd;
Gladsome hope shall spring above,
And shall bear the fruit of love.
To the Father, and the Son,
    And the Holy Ghost
Here be glory, as is done
    By the angelic host.

"Calls Thee by Thy Name"

God beholds thee individually, whoever thou art. He "calls thee by thy name." He sees thee, and understands thee, as He made thee. He knows what is in thee, all thy own peculiar feelings and thoughts, thy dispositions and likings, thy strength and thy weakness. He views thee in thy day of rejoicing, and thy day of sorrow. He sympathizes in thy hopes and thy temptations. He interests himself in all thy anxieties and remembrances, all the risings and fallings of thy spirit. He has numbered the very hairs of thy head and the cubits of thy stature. He compasses thee round and bears thee in His arms; He takes thee up and sets thee down. He notes thy very countenance, whether smiling or in tears, whether healthful or sickly. He looks tenderly upon thy hands and thy feet; He hears thy voice, the beating of thy heart, and thy very breathing. Thou dost not love thyself better than He loves thee. Thou canst not shrink from pain more than He dislikes thy bearing it; and if He puts it on thee, it is as thou would put it on thyself, if thou art wise, for a greater good afterwards. . . .

O my God, I will put myself without reserve into Thy hands. Wealth or woe, joy or sorrow, friends or bereavement, honor or humiliation, good report or ill report, comfort or discomfort, Thy presence or the hiding of Thy countenance, all is good if it comes from Thee. Thou art Wisdom and Thou art love— what can I desire more?

PRIMO DIE, QUO TRINITAS

Today the Blessed Three in One
    Began the earth and skies;
Today a Conqueror, God and Son,
    Did from the grave arise;
We too will wake, and, in despite
Of sloth and languor, all unite,
As Psalmists bid, through the dim night,
    Waiting with wistful eyes.
So may He hear, and heed each vow
    And prayer to Him addrest;

And grant an instant cleansing now,
    A future glorious rest.
So may He plentifully shower,
On all who hymn His love and power,
In this most still and sacred hour,
    His sweetest gifts and best.
Father of purity and light!
    Thy presence if we win,
'Twill shield us from the deeds of night,
    The burning darts of sin;
Lest aught defiled or dissolute
Relax our bodies or imbrute,
And fires eternal be the fruit
    Of fire now lit within.
Fix in our hearts, Redeemer dear,
    The ever-gushing spring
Of grace to cleanse, of life to cheer
    Souls sick and sorrowing.
Thee, bounteous Father, we entreat,
And Only Son, awful and sweet,
And life-creating Paraclete,
    The everlasting King.

FAITH IN THEE

The Son is in the Father and the Father in the Son. O adorable mystery which has been from eternity! I adore Thee, O my incomprehensible Creator, before whom I am an atom, a being of yesterday or an hour ago! Go back a few years, and I simply did not exist; I was not in being, and things went on without me:

but Thou art from eternity; and nothing whatever from one moment could go on without Thee. . . . O adorable mystery! Human reason has not conducted me to it, but I believe. I believe, because Thou hast spoken, O Lord. I joyfully accept Thy word about Thyself. Thou must know what Thou art—and who else? Not I surely, dust and ashes, except so far as Thou tellest me. I take then Thy own witness, O my Creator! and I believe firmly, I repeat after Thee, what I do not understand, because I wish to live a life of faith; and I prefer faith in Thee to trust in myself.

MY LORD GOD

He came to His disciples . . . walking upon the sea,—the emblem or hieroglyphic among the ancients of the impossible; to show them that what is impossible with man, is possible with God. He who could walk the waters, could also ride triumphantly upon what is still more fickle, unstable, tumultuous, treacherous—the billows of human wills, human purposes, human hearts.

My Lord God . . . I adore Thee. Thou art so mysterious, so incomprehensible. How can the Infinite be other than incomprehensible to me? Thou art without beginning . . . the only Eternal, who hast lived a whole eternity by Thyself who art all wisdom, all truth, all justice, all love, all holiness, all beautifulness, omniscient, omnipresent; absolutely perfect; and such, that what we do not know and can not even imagine of Thee, is far more wonderful than what we do and can. . . . Thou created all things out of nothing, and preservest them every moment, and couldst destroy them as easily as Thou madest them . . . a Being infinite yet personal; though the highest Thou makest Thyself as it were the servant of all. All we see, hear, touch, the remote sidereal firmament, as well as our own sea and land are Thine. All that is good, all that is true, all that is beautiful, all that is beneficent, be it great or small, be it perfect or fragmentary, natural as well as supernatural, moral as well as material, comes from Thee. . . .

It is my greatest stay to know that Thou readest my heart. O give me more of that open-hearted sincerity which I have desired. Keep me ever from being afraid of Thy eye, from the inward consciousness that I am not honestly trying to please Thee. Teach me to love Thee and then I shall be at peace, without any fear of Thee at all.

JAM LUCIS ORTO SIDERE
(From the Parisian Breviary)

Now that the day-star glimmers bright,
    We suppliantly pray
That He, the uncreated Light,
    May guide us on our way.

No sinful word, nor deed of wrong,
    Nor thoughts that idly rove;
But simple truth be on our tongue,
    And in our hearts be love.

And, while the hours in order flow,
    O Christ, securely fence
Our gates, beleaguer'd by the foe,—
    The gate of every sense.

And grant that to Thine honor,
    Lord, Our daily toil may tend;
That we begin it at Thy word,
    And in Thy blessing end.

And, lest the flesh in its excess
    Should lord it o'er the soul,
Let taming abstinence repress
    The rebel, and control.

To God the Father glory be,
    And to His Only Son,
And to the Spirit, One and Three,
    While endless ages run.

GOD AND MYSELF

Such is the great God, so all-sufficient, so all-blessed, so separate from creatures, so inscrutable, so unapproachable. Who can see Him? Who can fathom Him? Who can move Him? Who can even speak of Him? He is all-holy, all-patient, all-peaceful, and all-true. He says and He does; He delays and He executes; He warns and He punishes; He punishes, He rewards, He forbears, He pardons, according to an eternal decree, without imperfection, without vacillation, without inconsistency. . . .

Almighty God, Thou art the One Infinite Fulness. From eternity Thou art the one and only absolute and most all-sufficient seat and proper abode of all conceivable best attributes, and of all, which are many more, which cannot be achieved. I hold this as a matter of reason, though my imagination starts from it. I hold it firmly and absolutely, though it is the most difficult of all mysteries. I hold it from the actual experience of Thy blessings and mercies towards me, the evidence of Thy awful being and attributes, brought home continually to my reason, beyond the power of doubting or disputing. . . . I hold it because I could not bear to be without Thee. . . . I hold it from the terror of being left in this wild world without stay or protection. I hold it from humble love to Thee, from delight in Thy glory and exaltation, from my desire that Thou shouldst be great and the only great one. I hold it for Thy sake and because I love to think of Thee as so glorious, perfect, and beautiful. There is one God and none other but He. . . .

I see and know, O my good Jesus, that the only way in which I can possibly approach Thee in this world is the way of faith, faith in what Thou hast told me, and I thankfully follow this only way which Thou hast given me. Amen.

OFFER THEE

O Heart of Jesus, all love, I offer Thee these humble prayers for myself, and for all those who unite themselves with me in spirit to adore Thee. O holiest Heart of Jesus most lovely, I intend to renew and to offer to Thee these acts of adoration and these prayers, for myself a wretched sinner, and for all those who are associated with me in Thy adoration, through all moments while I breathe, even to the end of my life. I recommend to Thee, O my Jesus, Holy Church, Thy dear spouse, and our true Mother, all just souls and all poor sinners, the afflicted, the dying, and all mankind. Let not Thy Blood be shed for them in vain. Finally, deign to apply it in relief of the souls in Purgatory, of those in particular who have practised in the course of their life this holy devotion of adoring Thee.

SLAIN BY SIN

O tormented heart, it was love, and sorrow, and fear, which broke Thee. It was the sight of human sin, it was the sense of it, the feeling of it laid on Thee; it was zeal for the glory of God, horror at seeing sin so near Thee, a sickening, stifling feeling at its pollution, the deep shame and disgust and abhorrence and revolt which it inspired, keen pity for the souls whom it has drawn headlong into hell—all these feelings together Thou didst allow to rush upon Thee. Thou didst submit Thyself to their powers, and they were Thy death. That strong heart, that all-noble, all-generous, all-tender, all-pure heart was slain by sin. . . .

O Jesus, Son of Mary . . . we, after Thy pattern, would pray for all who are near and dear to us, and we beg Thy grace to do so continually. We beg Thee to bring them all into the light of Thy truth, or to keep them in Thy truth if they already know it. We thus pray for grandparents, quick and dead, for our fathers and our mothers, for our children, for every one of them, for our brothers and sisters, for our cousins and all our kindred, for our friends, and our father's friends, for all our old friends, for our dear and intimate friends, for our teachers, for our pupils, for our masters and employers, for our servants or subordinates, for our associates and work-fellows, for our neighbors, for our superiors and rulers; for those who wish us well; for those who wish us ill; for our enemies; for our rivals; for our injurers and for our slanderers. And not only for the living, but for the dead, who have died in the grace of God, that He may shorten their time of expiation, and admit them into His presence above.

RETURN TO THEE

The sun sinks to rise again; the day is swallowed up in the gloom of night, to be born out of it, as fresh as if it had never been quenched. Spring passes into summer, and through summer and autumn into winter, only the more surely, by its own ultimate return, to triumph over that grave, towards which it resolutely hastened from its first hour. We mourn over the blossoms of May, because they are to wither; but we know, withal, that May is one day to have its revenge upon November, by the revolution of that solemn circle which never stops—which teaches us in our height of hope, ever to be sober, and in our depth of desolation, never to despair. . . . O my God, shall I one day see Thee? What sight can compare to that great sight! Shall I see the source of that grace which enlightens me, strengthens me, and consoles me? As I came from Thee, as I am made through Thee, as I live in Thee, so, O my God, may I at last return to Thee, and be with Thee for ever and ever. . . . Eternal, Incomprehensible God, I believe, and confess, and adore Thee, as being infinitely more wonderful, resourceful, and immense, than this universe which I see. I look into the depths of space, in which the stars are scattered about, and I understand that I should be millions upon millions of years in creeping along from one end of it to the other, if a bridge were thrown across it. I consider the overpowering variety, richness, intricacy of Thy work; the elements, principles, laws, results which go to make it up. I should be ages upon ages in learning everything that is to be learned about this world, supposing me to have the power of learning it at all. And new sciences would come to light, at present unsuspected, as fast as I had mastered the old, and the conclusions of today would be nothing more than starting points of tomorrow. It is the occupation of eternity, ever new, inexhaustible, ineffably ecstatic, the stay and the blessedness of existence, thus to drink in and be dissolved in Thee. . . .

Since Thou art from everlasting, and hast created all things from a certain beginning, Thou hast lived in an eternity before Thou began to create anything. There was no earth, no sky, no sun, no space, no time, no beings of any kind; no men, no Angels, no Seraphim. Thy throne was without ministers; Thou were not waited on by any; all was silence, all was repose, there was nothing but God. Through a whole eternity Thou were by Thyself, with no other being but Thyself; blessed in Thyself and by Thyself, and wanting nothing. I cannot comprehend Thee more than I did, before I saw Thee on the Cross; but I have gained my lesson. I have before me the proof, that in spite of Thy awful nature, and the clouds and darkness that surround it, Thou canst think of me with a personal affection. Thou hast died that I might live. Amen.

ADORATION AYE BE GIVEN

Firmly I believe and truly
    God is Three, and God is One;
And I next acknowledge duly
    Manhood taken by the Son.
And I trust and hope most fully
    In that Manhood crucified;
And each thought and deed unruly
    Do to death, as He has died.
Simply to His grace and wholly
    Light and life and strength belong,
And I love, supremely, solely,
    Him the holy, Him the strong.
Sanctus fortis, Sanctus Deus,
    De profundis oro te,

Miserere Judex Meus,
    Parce mihi, Domine.
And I hold in veneration,
    For the love of Him alone,
Holy Church, as His creation,
    And her teachings, as His own.
And I take with joy whatever
    Now besets me, pain or fear,
And with a strong will I sever
    All the ties which bind me here.
Adoration aye be given,
    With and through the angelic host,
To the God of earth and Heaven,
    Father, Son, and Holy Ghost.

LOOK ON JESUS

Saint Paul tells us to "look on Jesus, the Author and Finisher of faith." Faith is the first step towards salvation, and without it we have no hope. For Saint Paul says, "Without Faith it is impossible to please God." It is a divine light; by it we are brought out of darkness into sunshine; by it, instead of groping, we are able to see our way toward heaven. . . .

O Lord Jesus Christ, upon the Cross Thou didst say: "Father forgive them, for they know not what they do." And this surely, O my God, is the condition of vast multitudes among us now; they know not what they might have known, or they have forgotten what once they knew. They mislead the wandering, they frighten the weak, they corrupt the young, but they know not what they do. O Lord, we urge Thee by Thy own dear word: Give them full and saving faith here; destroy their dreadful delusions, and give them to drink of that living water, which whoso hath shall not thirst again.

HIS GLORY

My Lord, I believe, and know, and feel, that Thou art the Supreme Good. And, in saying so, I mean, not only supreme Goodness and Benevolence, but that Thou art the sovereign and transcendent Beautifulness. I believe that, beautiful as is Thy creation, it is mere dust and ashes, and of no account, compared with Thee, who art the infinitely more beautiful Creator. Therefore it is that the Angels and Saints have such perfect bliss, because they see Thee. To see even the glimpse of Thy true glory, even in this world, throws holy men into an ecstasy. And I feel the truth of all this, in my own degree, because Thou hast mercifully taken our nature upon Thee, and hast come to me as man.—"And we saw His glory, the glory as it were of the only begotten of the Father." The more, O my dear Lord, I meditate on Thy words, works, actions, and sufferings in the Gospel, the more wonderfully glorious and beautiful I see Thee to be.

THAN LOSE THEE

And therefore, O my dear Lord, since I perceive Thee to be so beautiful, I love Thee, and desire to love Thee more and more. Since Thou art the One Goodness, Beautifulness, Gloriousness, in the whole world of being, and there is nothing like Thee, but Thou art infinitely more glorious and good than even the most beautiful of creatures, therefore I love Thee with a singular love, a one, only, sovereign love. After looking at Thee, there is nothing on earth, not even what is most naturally dear to me, that I can love in comparison of Thee. And I would lose everything whatever rather than lose Thee. For Thou, O my Lord, art my supreme and only Lord and love.

SOMNO REFECTIS ARTUBUS

Sleep has refresh'd our limbs, we spring
    From off our bed, and rise;
Lord, on Thy suppliants, while they sing,
    Look with a Father's eyes.

Be Thou the first on every tongue,
    The first in every heart;
That all our doings all day long,
    Holiest! from Thee may start.

Cleanse Thou the gloom, and bid the light
    Its healing beams renew;
The sins, which have crept in with night,
    With night shall vanish too.

Our bosoms, Lord, unburthen Thou,
    Let nothing there offend;

That those who hymn Thy praises now
   May hymn them to the end.

Grant this, O Father, Only Son,
   And Spirit, God of grace,
To whom all worship shall be done
   In every time and place.

ESPOUSAL

The love, O Lord Jesus Christ, which Thou inspirest lasts, for it is the love of the Unchangeable. It satisfies, for Thou art inexhaustible. The nearer we draw to Thee, the more triumphantly doest Thou enter into us; the longer Thou dwellest in us, the more intimately have we possession of Thee. It is an espousal for eternity. . . .

Everything short of Thee, O Lord, is changeable, but Thou endurest. Thou art ever one and the same. Ever the true God of man, and unchangeably so. Thou art the rarest, most precious, the sole good; and withal Thou art the most lasting. Thy creature changes, the Creator never. Then only the creature stops changing, when it rests on Thee. On Thee the angels look and are at peace; that is why they have perfect bliss. They never can lose their blessedness, for they never can lose Thee, "Jesus Christ, the same yesterday and today, Who is also forever." . . .

My Lord, my only God, let me never go after vanities. All is vanity and shadow here below. Let nothing allure me from Thee; keep me wholly and entirely. Draw me to Thee morning, noon, and night for consolation. Let me love Thee, O my Lord Jesus, with a pure affection and a fervent affection! Let me love Thee with the fervor, only greater, with which men of this earth love beings of this earth. Let me have that tenderness and constancy in loving Thee, which is so much praised among men, when the object is of the earth. Let me find and feel Thee to be my only joy, my only refuge, my only strength, my only comfort, my only hope, my only fear, my only love. Amen.

THE ALL-BEAUTIFUL

Leave, then, the prison of your own reasonings, leave the town, the work of man, the haunt of sin; go forth, my brethren, far from the tents of Cedar and the slime of Babylon: with the patriarch go forth to meditate in the field, and from the splendors of the work imagine the unimaginable glory of the Architect. Mount some bold eminence, and look back, when the sun is high and full upon the earth, when mountains, cliffs, and sea rise up before you like a brilliant pageant, with outlines noble and graceful, and tints and shadows soft, clear, and harmonious, giving depth, and unity to the whole; and then go through the forest, or beautiful field, or along meadows and stream, and listen to the distant country sounds, and drink in the fragrant air which is poured around you in spring or summer; or go among the gardens, and delight your senses with the grace and splendor, and the various sweetness of the flowers you find there; then think of the almost mysterious influence upon the mind of particular scents, or the emotion which some gentle, peaceful strain excites in us, or how soul and body are rapt and carried away captive by the concord of musical sounds, when the ear is open to their power; and then, when you have ranged through sights, sounds, and odors, and your heart kindles, and your voice is full of praise and worship, reflect—not that they tell you nothing of their Maker,—but that they are the poorest and dimmest glimmerings of His glory, and the very refuse of His exuberant riches, and but the dusky smoke which precedes the flame, compared with Him who made them. Such is the Creator in His Eternal Uncreated Beauty, that, were it given to us to behold it, we should die of very rapture at the sight. Moses, unable to forget the token of it he had once seen in the bush, asked to see it fully, and on this very account was refused. "He said, Show me Thy glory; and He said Thou canst not see My Face; for man shall not see me and live." When saints have been favored with glimpses of it, it has thrown them into ecstasy, broken their poor frames of dust and ashes, and pierced them through with such keen distress, that they have cried out to God, in the very midst of their transports, that He would hold His hand, and, in tenderness to them, check the abundance of His consolations.

What saints partake in fact, I enjoy in thought and imagination; and even that mere reflection of Thy glory, my God, is sufficient to sweep away all gloomy, envious thoughts, which circle around me, and lead me to forget myself in the contemplation of Thee, the All-beautiful. Thou art so bright, so majestic, so serene, so harmonious, so pure; Thou so surpassest, as being its archetype and fulness, all that is graceful, gentle, sweet, and fair on earth; Thy voice is so touching, and Thy smile so winning while so awful, that I need nothing more than to gaze and listen, and be happy.

RECTOR POTENS, VERAX DEUS

O God, who canst not change nor fail,
    Guiding the hours, as they roll by,
Bright'ning with beams the morning pale,
    And burning in the mid-day sky,

Quench Thou the fires of hate and strife,
    The wasting fever of the heart;
From perils guard our feeble life,
    And to our souls Thy peace impart.

Grant this, O Father, Only Son,
    And Holy Spirit, God of grace,
To whom all glory, Three in One,
    Be given in every time and place.

CONTEMPLATE THEE

I adore Thee, my God, as having laid down the ends and the means of all things which Thou hast created. Thou hast created everything for some end of its own, and Thou dost direct it to that end. The end, which Thou didst in the beginning appoint for man, is Thy worship and service, and his own happiness in paying it; a blessed eternity of soul and body with Thee for ever. Thou hast provided for this, and that in the case of every man. As Thy hand and eye are upon the brute creation, so are they upon us. Not a reptile, not an insect, but Thou seest and makest to live, while its time lasts. Not a sinner, not an idolater, not a blasphemer, not an atheist lives, but by Thee, and in order that he may repent. Thou art careful and tender to each of the beings that Thou hast created, as if it were the only one in the whole world. For Thou canst see every one of them at once, and Thou lovest every one in this mortal life, and pursuest every one by itself, with all the fulness of Thy attributes, as if Thou wast waiting on it and ministering to it for its own sake. My God, I love to contemplate Thee, I love to adore Thee, Thou the wonderful worker of all things every day in every place.

ALL THY ACTS OF PROVIDENCE

All Thy acts of Providence are acts of love. If Thou sendest evil upon us, it is in love. All the evils of the physical world are intended for the good of Thy creatures, or are the unavoidable attendants on that good. And Thou turnest that evil into good. Thou visitest men with evil to bring them to repentance, to increase their virtue, to gain for them greater good hereafter. Nothing is done in vain, but has its gracious end. Even Thy justice is mercy to others, as saving them from contamination, or granting them a warning. I acknowledge with a full and firm faith, O Lord, the wisdom and goodness of Thy Providence, even in Thy inscrutable judgments and Thy incomprehensible decrees.

SERENE JOY

May I watch and wait for Thee, Lord, be ever tender and sensitive in my devotion towards Thee; ever feed on the thought of Thee, hang on Thy words; live in Thy smile, and thrive and grow under Thy hand; ever be eager for Thy approval, quick in catching Thy meaning, jealous of Thy honor; ever see Thee in all things, expect Thee in all events, and amid all the cares, the interests, and the pursuits of this life, truly feel a serene joy, not a disappointment, did I hear that Thou wast on the point of coming.

. . . For centuries before Thou camest on earth, prophet after prophet was upon his high tower, looking out for Thee through the thick night, and watching for the faintest glimmer of the dawn. The martyrs, the confessors of the Church, bishops, evangelists, doctors, preachers, monks, hermits, ascetical teachers lived on Thy very name of Jesus, as food, as medicine, as fragrance, as light, as life from the dead. May I cease to be an exception in Thy great family, which is ever adoring, praising, and loving Thee. Amen.

To Lead Me

Ten thousand difficulties do not make one doubt.... A man may be annoyed that he cannot work out a mathematical problem, of which the answer is or is not given to him, without doubting that it admits of an answer, or that a certain particular answer is the true one....

Make me what Thou wouldst have me; I bargain for nothing; I make no terms; I seek for no previous information whither Thou art taking me; I will be what Thou wilt make me, and all that Thou wilt make me. I say not, I will follow Thee withersoever Thou goest, for I am weak; but I give myself to Thee, to lead me anywhither.

I Have My Mission

God has created me to do Him some definite service; He has committed some work to me which He has not committed to another. I have my mission—I never may know it in this life, but I shall be told it in the next. Somehow I am necessary for His purposes, as necessary in my place as an Archangel in his. If, indeed, I fail, He can raise another, as He could make the stones children of Abraham. Yet I have a part in this great work; I am a link in a chain, a bond of connexion between persons. He has not created me for naught. I shall do good, I shall do His work; I shall be an angel of peace, a preacher of truth in my own place, while not intending it, if I do but keep His commandments and serve Him in my calling....

O Adonai, O Ruler of Israel, Thou that guidest Joseph like a flock, O Emmanuel, O Sapientia, I give myself to Thee. I trust Thee wholly. Thou art wiser than I—more loving to me than I myself. Deign to fulfil Thy high purposes in me whatever they be— work in and through me. I am born to serve Thee, to be Thine, to be Thy instrument. Let me be Thy blind instrument. I ask not to see—I ask not to know—I ask simply to be used.

THAT HUMAN NATURE

O dear Lord . . . Thou so lovest this human nature which Thou hast created. Thou didst not love us merely as Thy creatures, the work of Thy hands, but as men. Thou lovest all, for Thou hast created all; but Thou lovest man more than all. How is it, Lord, that this should be? What is there in man above others? "What is man, that Thou art mindful of him?" . . . "nowhere doth he take hold of the angels." Who can sound the depth of Thy counsels and decrees? Thou hast loved man more than Thou hast loved the angels: and therefore, as Thou didst not take on Thee an angelic nature when Thou didst manifest Thyself for our salvation, so too Thou wouldst not come in any shape or capacity or office which was above the course of ordinary human life—not as a Nazarene, not as a Levitical priest, not as a monk, not as a hermit, but in the fullness and exactness of that human nature which so much Thou lovest.

Thou camest not only a perfect man, but as proper man; not formed anew out of earth, not with the spiritual body which Thou now hast, but in that very flesh which had fallen in Adam, and with all our infirmities, all our feelings and sympathies, sin excepted.

MY ELDER BROTHER

O Jesus, it became Thee, the great God, thus abundantly and largely to do Thy work, for which the Father sent Thee. Thou didst not do it by halves—and, while that magnificence of Sacrifice is Thy glory as God, it is our consolation and aid as sinners. O dearest Lord, Thou art more fully man than the holy Baptist, than Saint John, Apostle and Evangelist, than Thy own sweet Mother. As in Divine knowledge of me Thou art beyond them all, so also in experience and personal knowledge of my nature. Thou art my elder brother. How can I fear, how should I not repose my whole heart on one so gentle, so tender, so familiar, so unpretending, so modest, so natural, so humble? Thou art now, though in heaven, just the same as Thou wast on earth; the mighty God, yet the little child—the all-holy, yet the all-sensitive, all-human.

EN CLARA VOX REDARGUIT

Hark, a joyful voice is thrilling,
    And each dim and winding way
Of the ancient Temple filling;
    Dreams, depart! for it is day.

Christ is coming!—from thy bed,
    Earth-bound soul, awake and spring,—
With the sun new-risen to shed
    Health on human suffering.

Lo! to grant a pardon free,
    Comes a willing Lamb from Heaven;
Sad and tearful, hasten we,
    One and all, to be forgiven.

Once again He comes in light,
    Girding each with fear and woe:
Lord! be Thou our loving Might,
    From our guilt and ghostly foe.

To the Father, and the Son,
    And the Spirit, who in Heaven
Ever witness, Three and One,
    Praise on earth be ever given.

As Their Father

All below heaven changes: spring, summer, autumn, each has its turn. The fortunes of the world change; what was high, lies low; what was low, rises high. Riches take wing and flee away; bereavements happen. Friends become enemies, and enemies friends. Our wishes, aims and plans change. There is nothing stable but Thou, O my God! And Thou art the center and life of all who change, who trust Thee as their Father, who look to Thee and are content to put themselves into Thy hands.

Lux Alma Jesu

Light of the anxious heart,
  Jesus, Thou dost appear,
To bid the gloom of guilt depart,
  And shed Thy sweetness here.

Joyous is he, with whom,
  God's Word, Thou dost abide;
Sweet Light of our eternal home,
  To fleshly sense denied.

Brightness of God above!
  Unfathomable grace!
Thy Presence be a fount of love
  Within Thy chosen place.

To Thee, whom children see,
  The Father ever blest,
The Holy Spirit, One and Three,
  Be endless praise addresst. Amen.

With the Eyes of the Spirit

"His head and hairs are white like white wool, and as snow"—Thy hair is white, O Jesus, because Thou art the Ancient of Days, as the Prophet Daniel speaks. From everlasting to everlasting Thou art God. Thou didst come indeed to us as a little child—Thou didst hang upon the Cross at an age of life before as yet grey hairs come—but, O my dear Lord, there was always something mysterious about Thee, so that men

were not quite sure of Thy age. The Pharisees talk-
ed of Thee as near fifty. And even when Thou wast a
child, Thy hair shone so bright that people said "It is
snow." O my Lord Thou art ever old, and ever young.
Thou hast all perfection, and old age in Thee is ten
thousand times more beautiful than the most beautiful youth. Thy white hair is an ornament, not a sign
of decay. It is as dazzling as the sun, as white as the
light, and as glorious as gold. Jesus may I ever love
Thee, not with human eyes, but with the eyes of the
spirit, which sees not as man sees.

IMMENSE COELI CONDITOR

Lord of unbounded space,
 Who, lest the sky and main
Should mix, and heaven should lose its place,
 Didst the rude waters chain;

Parting the moist and rare,
 That rills on earth might flow
To soothe the angry flame, whene'er
 It ravens from below;

Pour on us of Thy grace
 The everlasting spring;
Lest our frail steps renew the trace
 Of the ancient wandering.

May faith in luster grow,
 And rear her star in heaven,

Paling all sparks of earth below,
Unquench'd by damps of even.

Grant it, O Father, Son,
And Holy Spirit of grace,
To whom be glory, Three in One,
In every time and place.

A Confiteor

I will raise my voice, and chant a perpetual Confiteor to Thee and to Thy Saints;—"to God Omnipotent, and to the Blessed Mary Ever-Virgin," (Thy Mother and mine, immaculate in her conception), "and to blessed Michael," (created in his purity by the very hand of God), and "to Blessed John the Baptist," (sanctified even in his mother's womb); and after these three, "to the Holy Apostles Peter and Paul," (penitents, who compassionate the sinner from their experience of sin); "to all the saints," (whether they have lived in contemplation or in toil, during the days of their pilgrimage), to all the saints will I address my supplication, that they may "remember me, since it is well with them, and do mercy by me, and make mention of me unto the King that He bring me out of prison." And then at length "God shall wipe away every tear from my eyes, and death shall be no longer, nor mourning nor crying, nor pain any more, for the former things are passed away."

COELI DEUS SANCTISSIME

O Lord, who, thron'd in the holy height,
    Through plains of ether didst diffuse
      The dazzling beams of light,
        In soft transparent hues;

Who didst, on the fourth day, in heaven
    Light the fierce cresset of the sun,
      And the meek moon at even,
        And stars that wildly run;

That they might mark and arbitrate
    'Twixt alternating night and day,
      And tend the train sedate
        Of months upon their way;

Clear, Lord, the brooding night within,
    And clean these hearts for Thy abode,
      Unlock the spell of sin,
        Crumble its giant load.
Grant it, O Father, Only Son,
    And Holy Spirit, God of Grace,
      To whom all praise be done
        In every time and place.

OTHER PARTAKERS

What things ought we to render to Almighty God that He has made us what we are! It is a matter of grace. . . . You are then what you are, not from any excellence or merit of your own, but by the grace of God who has chosen you to believe. Has He not visited you with over-abundant grace? And was it not necessary for your hard hearts to receive more than other people? Praise and bless Him continually for the benefit; do not forget, as time goes on, that it is of grace; do not pride yourselves upon it, but pray ever not to lose it, and do your best to make others partakers of it.

When objections in matters of faith occur to me, which they may easily do as I live in the world, they are as odious and unwelcome to me as impure thoughts are to the virtuous. I shrink from them, I fling them away from me, but why? Not in the first instance, because they are dangerous, but because they are cruel and base. My loving Lord has done everything for me, and has He deserved such a return? "O my people, what have I done to thee, or in what have I afflicted thee? Answer thou Me."

Lord, Thou hast poured on me Thy grace. Thou hast been with me in my perplexities, Thou hast forgiven me my sins, Thou hast satisfied my reason, Thou hast made faith easy, Thou hast given me Thy saints, Thou showest before me day after day Thy own Passion; why should I leave Thee? What hast Thou ever done to me but good? . . .

Shine forth, O Lord, as when on Thy Nativity Thine Angels visited the shepherds; let Thy glory blossom forth as bloom and foliage on the trees; change with Thy mighty power this visible world into that diviner world, which as yet we see not; destroy what we see, that it may pass and be transferred into what we believe. We know that what we see is as a screen hiding from us Jesus Christ and His Saints and Angels. Lord, we earnestly desire and pray for the dissolution of all that we see, from our longing after that which we do not see. Amen.

TELLURIS ALME CONDITOR

All-Bountiful Creator, Who,
    When Thou didst mould the world, didst drain
The waters from the mass, that so
    Earth might immovable remain;

That its dull clods it might transmute
    To golden flowers in vale or wood,
To juice of thirst allaying fruit,
    And grateful herbage spread for food;

Wash Thou our smarting wounds and hot,
    In the cool freshness of Thy grace;
Till tears start forth the past to blot,
    And cleanse and calm Thy holy place;

Till we obey Thy full behest,
    Shun the world's tainted touch and breath,
Joy in what highest is and best,
    And gain a spell to baffle death.

Grant it, O Father, only Son,
    And Holy Spirit, God of grace;
To whom all glory, Three in One,
    Be given in every time and place.

RAISE MY HEART

O my God, whatever is nearer to me than Thou, things of this earth, and things more naturally pleasing to me, will be sure to interrupt the sight of Thee, unless Thy grace interfere. Keep Thou my eyes, my ears, my heart, from any such miserable tyranny. Keep my whole being fixed on Thee. Let me never lose sight of Thee; and while I gaze on Thee, let my love of Thee grow more and more every day.

RABBONI

Let me ever hold communion with Thee, my hidden but my living God. Thou art my innermost heart. Thou art the life of my life. Every breath I breathe, every thought of my mind, every good desire of my heart, is from the presence within me of the unseen God. I see Thee not in the material world except dimly, but I recognize Thy voice in my own intimate consciousness. I turn round and say *Rabboni*. O be ever thus with me; and if I am tempted to leave Thee, do not Thou, O my God, leave me!

IN MY EVIL HOUR OF TEMPTATION

Rescue me, my Lord, in this my evil hour,
As of old so many by Thy gracious power:
    (Amen.)
Enoch and Elias from the common doom;
    (Amen.)
Noe from the waters in a saving home;
    (Amen.)

Abraham from th' abounding guilt of Heathenesse;
  (Amen.)
Job from all his multiform and fell distress;
  (Amen.)
Isaac, when his father's knife was raised to slay;
  (Amen.)
Lot from burning Sodom on its judgment-day;
  (Amen.)
Moses from the land of bondage and despair;
  (Amen.)
Daniel from the hungry lions in their lair;
  (Amen.)
And the children three amid the furnace-flame;
  (Amen.)
Chaste Susanna from the slander and the shame;
  (Amen.)
David from Goliath and the wrathful Saul;
  (Amen.)
And the two Apostles from their prison-thrall;
  (Amen.)
Thecia from her torments;
  (Amen.)
. . . so, to show Thy Power,
Rescue me Thy servant in my evil hour.
  (Amen.)

THY SOLDIERS

O Lion of the Tribe of Judah, the root of David, who fightest the good fight, and hast called on all men to join Thee, give Thy courage and strength to all

Thy soldiers over the whole earth, who are fighting under the standard of Thy cross. Be with Thy missionaries in pagan lands, put right words into their mouths, prosper their labors, and sustain them under their sufferings with Thy consolations, and carry them on, even through torments and blood (if it be necessary), to their reward in Heaven. Amen.

LOYALTY TO THEE

O my God, my whole life has been a course of mercies and blessings shown to one who has been most unworthy of them. I require no faith, for I have had long experience, as to Thy Providence toward me. Year after year Thou hast carried me on, removed dangers from my path, recovered me, recruited me, refreshed me, borne with me, directed me, sustained me. O forsake me not when my strength faileth me. And Thou never wilt forsake me. I may rest upon Thy arm; I may go to sleep in Thy bosom. Only give me, and increase in me, that true loyalty to Thee, which is the bond of the covenant between Thee and me, and the pledge in my own heart and conscience that Thou, the Supreme God, wilt not forsake me, the most miserable of Thy children.

THE GRACE OF THY LOVE

O my God, strengthen me with Thy strength, console me with Thy everlasting peace, soothe me with the beauty of Thy countenance; enlighten me with Thy uncreated brightness; purify me with the fragrance of Thy ineffable holiness. Bathe me in Thyself and give me to drink, as far as mortal man may ask, of the rivers of grace which flow from the Father and the Son, the grace of Thy consubstantial, coeternal Love. Amen.

WE SHALL BE GLAD

Lord, Thou hast been our refuge: in every
     generation;
Before the hills were born, and the world was: from
     age to age Thou art God.
Bring us not, Lord, very low: for Thou hast said,
     come back again, ye sons of Adam.
A thousand years before Thine eyes are but as
     yesterday: and as a watch of the night which
     is come and gone.
The grass springs up in the morning: at eveningtide
     it shrivels up and dies.
So we fail in Thine anger: and in Thy wrath we are
     troubled.
Thou hast set our sins in Thy sight: and our round of
     days in the light of Thy countenance.
Come back, O Lord! How long: and be entreated for
     Thy servants.
In Thy morning we shall be filled with Thy mercy:
     we shall rejoice and be in pleasure all our
     days.
We shall be glad according to the days of our
     humiliation: and the years in which we have
     seen evil.

Look, O Lord, upon Thy servants and on Thy work:
    and direct Thy children.
And let the beauty of the Lord our God be upon us:
    and the work of our hands, establish Thou it.
(Glory be to the Father, and to the Son: and to the
    Holy Ghost.
As it was in the beginning, is now, and ever shall be:
    world without end. Amen.)

Nocte Surgentes

Let us arise, and watch by night,
    And meditate always,
And chant, as in our Maker's sight,
    United hymns of praise.

So, singing with the saints in bliss,
    With them we may attain
Life everlasting after this,
    And heaven for earthly pain.

Grant this, O Father, Only Son,
    And Spirit, God of grace,
To whom all worship shall be done
    In every time and place.

"Jesus Wept"

He wept from very sympathy with the grief of others. "Jesus, therefore, when he saw Mary weeping, and the Jews that were come with her, weeping, groaned in the spirit, and troubled himself." It is the very nature of compassion or sympathy, as the word implies, to "rejoice with those who rejoice, and weep with those who weep." We know it is so with men; and God tells us He also is compassionate, and full of tender mercy. Yet we do not well know what this means, for how can God rejoice or grieve? By the very perfection of His nature Almighty God cannot show sympathy, at least to the comprehension of beings of such limited minds as ours. He, indeed, is hid from us; but if we were allowed to see Him, how could we discern in the Eternal and Unchangeable signs of sympathy? Words and works of sympathy He does display to us; but it is the very sight of sympathy in another that affects and comforts the sufferer more even than the fruits of it. Now we cannot see God's sympathy; and the Son of God, though feeling for us as great compassion as His Father, did not show it to us while He remained in His Father's bosom. But when He took flesh and appeared on earth, He showed us the Godhead in a new manifestation, taking a human soul and body, in order that thoughts, feelings, affections, might be His, which could respond to ours and certify to us His tender mercy. When, then, our Saviour weeps from sympathy at Mary's tears, it is the love of God, the compassion of the Almighty and Eternal, condescending to appear as we are capable of receiving it, in the form of human tears.

Jesus wept, therefore, not merely from the deep thoughts of His understanding, but from spontaneous tenderness; from the gentleness and mercy, the encompassing loving-kindness and exuberant fostering affection of the Son of God for His own work, the race of man. Their tears touched Him at once, as their miseries had brought Him down from Heaven. His ear was open to them, and the sound of weeping went at once to His heart.

Till Thou Art Seen

Unveil, O Lord, and on us shine,
In glory and in grace;
This gaudy world grows dim before
The beauty of Thy face.

Till Thou art seen, it seems to be
A sort of fairy ground,
Where suns unsetting light the sky,
And flowers and fruits abound.

But when Thy keener, purer beam
Is poured upon our sight,
It loses all its power to charm,
And what was day, is night.

Its noblest toils are then the scourge
Which made Thy blood to flow:
Its joys are but the treacherous thorns
Which circled round Thy brow.

And thus, when we renounce for Thee
Its restless aims and fears,
The tender memories of the past,

The hopes of coming years,

Poor is our sacrifice, whose eyes
Are lighted from above;
We offer what we cannot keep,
What we have ceased to love.

— II. —

Our Lord's Sufferings

And we begin, by degrees, to perceive
that there are but two beings in
the whole universe, our own soul,
and the God who made it.

To Suffer and to Die

Praise to the Holiest in the height,
  And in the depth be praise:
In all His words most wonderful;
  Most sure in all His ways!

O loving wisdom of our God!
  When all was sin and shame,
A second Adam to the fight
  And to the rescue came.

O wisest love! that flesh and blood
  Which did in Adam fail,
Should strive afresh against the foe,
  Should strive and should prevail;

And that a higher gift than grace
  Should flesh and blood refine,
God's Presence and His very Self,
  And Essence all divine.

O generous love! that He who smote
  In man for man the foe,
The double agony in man
  For man should undergo;

And in the garden secretly,
  And on the cross on high,
Should teach His brethren and inspire
  To suffer and to die.

O Wayward Man!

"Who is this that cometh from Edom, with dyed garments from Bozra? Why is thy apparel red, and thy garments like theirs that tread in the wine press?" It is because the maker of man, the Wisdom of God, has come, not in strength but in weakness. He has come, not to assert a claim, but to pay a debt. Instead of wealth, He has come poor; instead of honor, He has come to ignominy; instead of blessedness, He has come to suffer. He has been delivered over from His birth to pain and contempt; His delicate frame is worn down by cold and heat, by hunger and sleeplessness; His hands are rough and bruised with a mechanic's toil; His eyes are dimmed with weeping; His name is cast out as evil. He is flung amid the throng of men; He wanders from place to place; He is the companion of sinners. He is followed by a mixed multitude, who care more for meat and drink than for His teaching, or by a city's populace which deserts Him in the day of trial. And at length "the Brightness of God's Glory and the Image of His Substance" is fettered, haled to and fro, buffeted, spit upon, mocked, cursed, scourged, and tortured. "He hath no beauty, no comeliness; He is despised and the most abject of men, Man of sorrows and acquainted with infirmity"; nay, He is a "leper, and smitten of God, and afflicted." And so His clothes are torn off, and He is lifted up upon the bitter cross, and there He hangs, a spectacle for profane, impure, and savage eyes, and a mockery for the evil spirit whom He had cast down into hell.

O wayward man! discontented first that my God is far from me, discontented again when He has drawn near me,—complaining first that He is high, complaining next that He is low!—unhumbled being, when wilt I cease to make myself my own center and learn that God is infinite in all He does, infinite when He reigns in heaven, infinite when He serves on earth, exacting my homage in the midst of His angels and winning homage from me in the midst of sinners?

THE AGONY IN THE GARDEN
(A Meditation)

There, then, in that most awful hour, knelt the Savior of the world, putting off the defenses of His divinity, dismissing His reluctant angels, who in myriads were ready at His call, and opening His arms, bearing His breast, sinless as He was, to the assault of His foe—of a foe whose breath was a pestilence, and whose embrace was an agony. There He knelt, motionless and still, while the vile and horrible fiend clad His spirit in a robe steeped in all that is hateful and heinous in human crime, which clung close round His heart, and filled His conscience, and found its way into every sense and pore of His mind, and spread over Him a moral leprosy, till He almost felt Himself to be that which He never could be, and which His foe would fain have made Him. Oh, the horror, when He looked, and did not know Himself, and felt as a foul and loathsome sinner, from His vivid perception of that mass of corruption which poured over His head and ran down even to the skirts of His garments! Oh, the distraction, when He found His eyes, and hands, and feet and lips, and heart, as if the members of the Evil One, and not of God! Are these the hands of the Immaculate Lamb of God, once innocent, but now red with ten thousand barbarous deeds of blood? are these His lips, not uttering prayer, and praise, and holy blessings, but as if defiled with oaths, and blasphemies, and doctrines of devils? or His eyes, profaned as they are by all the evil visions and idolatrous fascinations for which men have abandoned their adorable Creator? And His ears, they ring with sounds of revelry and of strife; and His heart is frozen with avarice, and cruelty and unbelief; and His very memory is laden with every sin which has been committed since the fall, in all regions of the earth, with the pride of the old giants, and the lusts of the five cities, and the obduracy of Egypt, and the ambition of Babel, and the unthankfulness and scorn of Israel. Oh, who does not know the misery of a haunting thought which comes again and again, in spite of rejection, to annoy if it cannot seduce? or of some odious and sickening imagination, in no sense one's own, but forced upon the mind from without? or of evil knowledge, gained with or without a man's fault, but which he would give a great price to be rid of at once and forever? And adversaries such as these gather around Thee, Blessed Lord, in millions now; they come in troops more numerous than the locust or the palmer-worm, or the plagues of hail, and flies, and frogs, which were sent against Pharaoh. Of the living and of the dead and of the as yet unborn, of the lost and of the saved, of Thy people and of strangers, of sinners and of saints, all sins are there. Thy dearest are there, Thy saints and Thy chosen are upon Thee; Thy three Apostles, Peter, James and John; but not as comforters, but as accusers, like the friends of Job, "sprinkling dust toward heaven," "and heaping curses on Thy head." All are there but one; one only is not there, the only; for she who had no part in sin, she only could console Thee, and therefore she is not nigh. She will be near Thee on the Cross, she is separated from Thee in the garden. She has been Thy companion and Thy confidant through Thy life, she interchanged with Thee the pure thoughts and holy meditations of thirty years; but her virgin ear may not take in, nor may her immaculate heart conceive, what now is in vision before Thee. None was equal to the weight but God; sometimes before Thy saints Thou hast brought the image of a single sin, as it appears in the light of Thy countenance, or of venial sins, not mortal; and they have told us that the sight did all but kill them, nay would have killed them, had it not been instantly withdrawn. The Mother of God, for all her sanctity, nay by reason of it, could not have borne even one brood of that innumerable progeny of Satan which now compasses Thee about. It is the long history of the world, and God alone can bear the load of it. Hopes blighted, vows broken, lights quenched, warnings scorned, opportunities lost; the innocent betrayed, the young hardened, the penitent relapsing, the just overcome, the aged failing; the sophistry of misbelief, the willfulness of passion, the obduracy of pride, the tyranny of habit, the canker of remorse, the wasting fever of care, the anguish of shame, the pining of disappointment, the sickness of despair; such cruel, such pitiable spectacles, such heartrending, revolting, detestable, maddening scenes; nay, the haggard faces, the convulsed lips, the flushed cheek, the dark brow of the willing slaves of evil, they are all before Him now; they are upon Him and in Him. They are with Him instead of that ineffable peace which has inhabited His soul since the moment of His conception. They are upon Him, they are all but His own; He cries to His Father as if He were the criminal, not the victim; His agony takes the form of guilt and compunction.

My God, Thou art doing penance, Thou art making confession, Thou art exercising contrition, with a reality and a virtue infinitely greater than that of all saints and penitents together; for Thou art the One Victim of us all, the sole Satisfaction, the real Penitent, all but the real sinner.

Nox Atra Rerum Contegit

All tender light, all hues divine
 The night has swept away;
Shine on us, Lord, and we shall shine
 Bright in an inward day.

The spots of guilt, sin's wages base,
　　Searcher of hearts, we own;
Wash us and robe us in Thy grace,
　　Who didst for sins atone.

The sluggard soul, that bears their mark,
　　Shrinks in its silent lair,
Or gropes amid its chambers dark
　　For Thee, Who art not there.

Redeemer! send Thy piercing rays,
　　That we may bear to be
Set in the light of Thy pure gaze,
　　And yet rejoice in Thee.

Grant this, O Father, Only Son,
　　And Spirit, God of grace,
To whom all worship shall be done
　　In every time and place.

The Stations: I

"With Christ I am nailed to
the cross." (Gal 2:20)

I. Who Signed It?

Leaving the house of Caiphas, and dragged before
Pilate and Herod, mocked, beaten, and spit upon,
His back torn with scourges, His head crowned with
thorns, Jesus, Who on the last day will judge the
world, is Himself condemned by unjust judges to a
death of ignominy and torture.

Jesus is condemned to *death*. His death-warrant
is signed, and who signed it but I, when I committed my first mortal sins? My first mortal sins, when
I fell away from the state of grace into which Thou
didst place me by baptism; these it was that were Thy
death-warrant, O Lord. The innocent suffered for the
guilty. Those sins of mine were the voices which
cried out, "Let Him be crucified"; were the consent
which Pilate gave to this clamorous multitude. And
the hardness of heart which followed upon them,
my disgust, my despair, my proud impatience, my
obstinate resolve to sin on, the love of sin which
took possession of me—what were these contrary
and impetuous feelings but the blows and the blasphemies with which the fierce soldiers and the populace received Thee, thus carrying out the sentence
which Pilate had pronounced?

II. The Weight of Our Sins

A strong, and therefore heavy cross, for it is strong enough to bear Him on it when He arrives at Calvary, is placed upon His torn shoulders. He receives it gently and meekly, nay, with gladness of heart, for it is to be the salvation of mankind.

True; but recollect, that heavy cross is the weight of our sins. As it fell upon His neck and shoulders, it came down with a shock. Alas! What a sudden, heavy weight have I laid upon Thee, O Jesus. And, though in the calm and clear foresight of Thy mind—for Thou seest all things—Thou wast fully prepared for it, yet Thy feeble frame tottered under it when it dropped down upon Thee.

I have lifted up my hand against my God. How could I ever fancy He would forgive me unless He had Himself told us that He underwent His bitter passion in order that He might forgive us. I acknowledge, O Jesus, and anguish in the agony of my heart, that my sins it was that struck Thee on the face, that bruised Thy sacred arms, that tore Thy flesh with iron rods, that nailed Thee to the cross, and let Thee slowly die upon it.

III. Into Mortal Sin

Jesus, bowed down under the weight and the length of the unwieldy cross, which trailed after Him, slowly sets forth on His way, amid the mockeries and insults of the crowd. His agony in the garden itself was sufficient to exhaust Him; but it was only the first of a multitude of sufferings. He sets off with His whole heart, but His limbs fail Him, and He falls.

Yes, it is as I feared. Jesus, the strong and mighty Lord, has found for the moment our sins stronger than Himself. He falls—yet He bore the load for a while; He tottered, but He bore up and walked onward. What, then, made Him give way? O my soul, thy falling back into mortal sin. I repented of the sins of my youth, and went on well for a time; but at length a new temptation came, when I was off my guard, and I suddenly fell away. Then all my good habits seemed to go at once; they were like a garment which is stripped off, so quickly and utterly did grace depart from me. And at that moment I looked at my Lord, and lo! He had fallen down, and I covered my face with my hands, and remained in a state of great confusion.

IV. SON AND MOTHER

Jesus rises; though wounded by His fall, He journeys on, with His cross still on His shoulders. He is bent down; but at one place, looking up, He sees His Mother. For an instant they just see each other, and He goes forward.

Mary would rather have had all His sufferings herself, could that have been, than not have known what they were by ceasing to be near Him. He, too, gained a refreshment, as from some soothing and grateful breath of air, to see her sad smile amid the sights and the noises which were about Him. She had known Him beautiful and glorious, with the freshness of Divine Innocence and peace upon His countenance; *now* she saw Him so changed and deformed that she could scarce have recognized Him, save for the piercing, thrilling, peace-inspiring look He gave her. Still, He was now carrying the load of the world's sins, and, all-holy though He was, He carried the image of them on His very face. He had been made sin for us, Who knew no sin; not a feature, not a limb, but spoke of guilt, of a curse, of punishment, of agony.

Oh, what a meeting of Son and Mother! Yet there was a mutual comfort, for there was a mutual sympathy. Jesus and Mary—do they forget that Passiontide through all eternity?

V. Simon of Cyrene

At length His strength fails utterly, and He is unable to proceed. The executioners stand perplexed. What are they to do? How is He to get to Calvary? Soon they see a stranger who seems strong and active—Simon of Cyrene. They seize on him, and compel him to carry the cross with Jesus. The sight of the Sufferer pierces the man's heart. Oh, what a privilege! O happy soul, elect of God! He takes the part assigned to him with joy.

This came of Mary's intercession. *He* prayed not for Himself, except that He might drink the full chalice of suffering and do His Father's will; but *she* showed herself a mother by following Him with her prayers, since she could help Him in no other way. She then sent this stranger to help Him. Sweet Mother, even *do* the like to us. Pray for us ever, Holy Mother of God, pray for us, whatever be our cross, as we pass along on our way. Pray for us, and we shall rise again, though we have fallen. Pray for us when sorrow, anxiety, or sickness comes upon us. Pray for us when we are prostrate under the power of temptation, and send some faithful servant of thine to succor us. And in the world to come, if found worthy to expiate our sins in the fiery prison, send some good angel to give us a season of refreshment. Pray for us, Holy Mother of God.

VI. VERONICA

As Jesus toils along up the hill, covered with the sweat of death, a woman makes her way through the crowd, and wipes His face with a napkin. In reward of her piety the cloth retains the impression of the Sacred Countenance upon it.

The relief which a Mother's tenderness secured is not yet all she did. Her prayers sent Veronica as well as Simon—Simon to do a man's work, Veronica to do the part of a woman. The devout servant of Jesus did what she could. As Magdalen had poured the ointment at the feast, so Veronica now offered Him this napkin in His passion. "Ah," she said, "would I could do more!" "Why have I not the strength of Simon, to take part in the burden of the cross? But men only can serve the Great High Priest, now that He is celebrating the solemn act of sacrifice."

O Jesus! Let us one and all minister to Thee according to our places and powers. And as Thou didst accept from Thy followers refreshment in Thy hour of trial, so give to us the support of Thy grace when we are hard pressed by our foe.

I feel I cannot bear up against temptation, weariness, despondency, and sin. I shall fall, O my dear Savior, I shall certainly fall, unless Thou dost renew for me my vigor like the eagle's, and breathe life into me by the soothing application and the touch of the holy sacraments which Thou hast appointed.

VII. I Fell from Thee

The pain of His wounds and the loss of blood increasing at every step of His way, again His limbs fail Him, and He falls on the ground.

What has He done to deserve all this? This is the reward received by the long-expected Messias from the Chosen People, the Children of Israel. I know what to answer. He falls because *I* have fallen. I have fallen again. I know well that without Thy grace, O Lord, I could not stand; and I fancied that I had kept closely to Thy sacraments; yet in spite of my going to Mass and to my duties, I am out of grace again. Why is it but because I have lost my devotional spirit, and have come to Thy holy ordinances in a cold, formal way, without inward affection. I thought the battle of life was over, and became secure. I had no lively faith, no sight of spiritual things. I ought to be a new creature, I ought to live by faith, hope, and charity; but I thought more of this world than the world to come—and at last I forgot that I was a servant of God, and followed the broad way that leadeth to destruction, not the narrow way which leadeth to life. And thus I fell from Thee.

VIII. WEEP FOR ME

At the sight of the sufferings of Jesus, the holy women are so pierced with grief that they cry out and bewail Him, careless what happens to them by so doing. Jesus, turning to them, said, "Daughters of Jerusalem, weep not over Me, but weep for yourselves and for your children."

Ah! can it be, O Lord, that *I* shall prove one of those sinful children for whom Thou biddest their mothers to weep. "Weep not for Me," He said, "for I am the Lamb of God, and am making atonement at My own will for the sins of the world. I am suffering now, but I shall triumph; and, when I triumph, those souls for whom I am dying, will either be my dearest friends or my deadliest enemies." Is it possible? O my Lord, can I grasp the terrible thought that Thou really didst weep for me—weep for me, as Thou didst weep over Jerusalem? Oh, withdraw not from me. I am in a very bad way. I have so much evil in me. I have so little of an earnest, brave spirit to set against that evil. O Lord, what will become of me? It is so difficult for me to drive away the evil spirit from my heart. Thou alone canst effectually cast him out.

IX. AGAIN HE FELL

Jesus had now reached almost to the top of Calvary; but, before He had gained the very spot where He was to be crucified, again He fell, and is again dragged up and goaded onward by the brutal soldiery.

We are told in Holy Scripture of three falls of Satan, the evil spirit. The first was in the beginning; the second, when the Gospel and the Kingdom of Heaven were preached to the world; the third will be at the end of all things. The first is told us by Saint John the Evangelist. He says: "There was a great battle in heaven. Michael and his angels fought with the dragon, and the dragon fought, and his angels. And they prevailed not, neither was their place found any more in heaven. And that great dragon was cast out, the old serpent, who is called the devil and Satan." The second fall, at the time of the Gospel, is spoken of by our Lord when He says, "I saw Satan, like lightning, falling from heaven." And the third by the same Saint John: "There came down fire from God out of the heaven . . . and the devil . . . was cast into the pool of fire and brimstone."

These three falls—the past, the present, and the future—the evil spirit had in mind when he moved Judas to betray our Lord. This was just his hour. Our Lord, when He was seized, said to His enemies, "This is your hour and the power of darkness." Satan knew his time was short, and thought he might use it to good effect. But little dreaming that he would be acting in behalf of the world's redemption, which our Lord's passion and death were to work out, in revenge, and, as he thought, in triumph, he smote Him once, he smote Him twice, he smote Him thrice, each successive time a heavier blow.

Our Lord's Sufferings | 59

This is the worst fall of the three. His strength has for a while utterly failed Him, and it is some time before the barbarous soldiers can bring Him to. Ah! it was His anticipation of what was to happen to me. I get worse and worse. He sees the end from the beginning. He was thinking of me all the time He dragged Himself along, up the Hill of Calvary. He saw that I should fall again in spite of all former warnings and former assistance. I thought my weakness lay all on one particular side which I knew. I had not a dream that I was not strong on the other. And so Satan came down on my unguarded side, and got the better of me from my self-trust and self-satisfaction. I was wanting in humility. I thought no harm would come on me, I thought I had outlived the danger of sinning; I thought it was an easy thing to get to heaven, and I was not watchful. It was my pride, and so I fell a third time.

X. THE HOLY OF HOLIEST

At length He has arrived at the place of sacrifice, and they begin to prepare Him for the cross. His garments are torn from His bleeding body, and He, the Holy of Holiest, stands exposed to the gaze of the coarse and scoffing multitude.

O Thou Who in Thy Passion wast stripped of all Thy clothes, and held up to the curiosity and mockery of the rabble, strip me of myself here and now, that in the Last Day I come not to shame before men and angels. Thou didst endure the shame on Calvary, that I might be spared the shame at the Judgment. Thou hadst nothing to be ashamed of personally, and the shame which Thou didst feel was because Thou hadst taken on Thee man's nature. When they took from Thee Thy garments, those innocent limbs of Thine were but objects of humble and loving adoration to the highest Seraphim. They stood around in speechless awe, wondering at Thy beauty, and they trembled at Thy infinite self-abasement. But I, O Lord, how shall I appear if Thou shalt hold me up hereafter to be gazed upon, stripped of that robe of grace which is Thine, and seen in my own personal life and nature? How shall I be fit for the society of angels, how for Thy presence, until Thou burnest this foul leprosy away in the fire of Purgatory?

XI. A Ransom for the World

The cross is laid on the ground, and Jesus stretched upon it, and then, swaying heavily to and fro, it is, after much exertion, jerked into the hole ready to receive it. Or, as others think, it is set upright, and Jesus is raised up and fastened to it. As the savage executioners drive in the huge nails, He offers Himself to the Eternal Father, as a ransom for the world. The blows are struck—the blood gushes forth.

With sweet modesty and gentleness toward the fierce rabble, stretching out His arms, as if He would embrace them, there He hung, a perplexity to the multitude, a terror to evil spirits, the wonder, the awe, yet the joy, the adoration of the holy angels.

XII. To Die to Sin

Jesus hung for three hours. During this time He prayed for His murderers, promised Paradise to the penitent robber, and committed His Blessed Mother to the guardianship of Saint John. Then all was finished, and He bowed His head and gave up His spirit.

The worst is over. The Holiest is dead and departed. The most tender, the most affectionate, the holiest of the sons of men is gone. Jesus is dead, and with His death my sin shall die. I protest once for all, before men and angels, that sin shall no more have dominion over me. The salvation of my soul shall be my first concern. With the aid of His grace I will create in me a deep hatred and sorrow for my past sins. I will try hard to detest sin, as much as I have ever loved it. Into God's hands I put myself, not by halves, but unreservedly. I promise Thee, O Lord, with the help of Thy grace, to keep out of the way of temptation, to avoid all occasions of sin, to turn at once from the voice of the Evil One, to be regular in my prayers, so to die to sin that Thou mayst not have died for me on the cross in vain.

XIII. In the Arms of Mary

The multitude have gone home; Calvary is left solitary and still, except that Saint John and the holy women are there. Then come Joseph of Arimathea and Nicodemus, and take down from the cross the body of Jesus, and place it in the arms of Mary.

O Mary, at last thou hast possession of thy Son. Now, when His enemies can do no more, they leave Him in contempt to thee. As His unexpected friends perform their difficult work, thou lookest on with unspeakable thoughts. Thy heart is pierced with the sword of which Simeon spoke. Without swooning, without trembling, thou dost receive Him to thy arms and on thy lap. Now thou art supremely happy as having Him, though He comes to thee not as He went from thee. He went from thy home, O Mother of God, in the strength and beauty of His manhood, and He comes back to thee dislocated, torn to pieces, mangled, dead. Yet, O Blessed Mary, thou art happier in this hour of woe than on the day of the marriage feast, for then He was leaving Thee, and now in the future, as a Risen Savior, He will be separated from thee no more.

XIV. Till the Hour Comes

But for a short three days, for a day and a half—Mary then must give Him up. He is not yet risen. His friends and servants take Him from thee, and place Him in an honorable tomb. They close it safely, till the hour comes for His resurrection.

Lie down and sleep in peace in the calm grave for a little while, dear Lord, and then wake up for an everlasting reign. We, like the faithful women, will watch around Thee, for all our treasure, all our life, is lodged with Thee. And, when our turn comes to die, grant, sweet Lord, that we may sleep calmly too, the sleep of the just. Let us sleep peacefully for the brief interval between death and the general resurrection. Let our friends remember us and pray for us, O dear Lord. Let Masses be said for us, so that the pains of Purgatory, so much deserved by us, and therefore so truthfully welcomed by us, may be over with little delay. Give us seasons of refreshment there; wrap us round with holy dreams and soothing contemplations, while we gather strength to ascend the heavens. And then let our faithful guardian angels help us up the glorious ladder, reaching from earth to heaven, which Jacob saw in vision. And when we reach the everlasting gates, let them open upon us with the music of angels; and let Saint Peter receive us, and our Lady, the glorious Queen of Saints, embrace us, and bring us to Thee, and to Thy Eternal Father, and to Thy Co-equal Spirit, Three Persons, One God, to reign with Them forever and ever.

LET US PRAY

God, who by the Precious Blood of Thy only-begotten Son didst sanctify the standard of the cross, grant, we beseech Thee, that all those who rejoice in the glory of the same holy cross, may at all times and places rejoice in Thy protection, through the same Christ, our Lord.

End with Pater, Ave, and Gloria, for the intention of the Sovereign Pontiff.

The Stations: II

I. Shall Judge the World

The holy, just, and true was judged by sinners, and put to death. Yet, while they judged, they were compelled to acquit Him. Judas, who betrayed Him, said, "I have sinned in that I have betrayed the innocent blood." Pilate, who sentenced Him, said, "I am innocent of the blood of this just person," and threw the guilt upon the Jews. The Centurion, who saw Him crucified, said, "Indeed this *was* a just man." Thus ever, O Lord, Thou art justified in Thy words, and dost overcome when Thou art judged. And so, much more, at the last day "they shall *look* on Him whom they pierced"; and He who was condemned in weakness shall judge the world in power, and even those who are condemned will confess their judgment is just.

II. Our Sins

Jesus supports the whole world by His divine power, for He is God; but the weight was less heavy than was the cross which our sins hewed out for Him. Our sins cost Him this humiliation. He had to take on Him our nature, and to appear among us as a man, and to offer up for us a great sacrifice. He had to pass a life in penance, and to endure His Passion and death at the end of it. O Lord God Almighty, Who dost bear the weight of the whole world without weariness, who borest the weight of all our sins, though they wearied Thee, as Thou art the Preserver of our bodies by Thy Providence, so be Thou the Savior of our souls by Thy Precious Blood.

III. OUT OF SIN

Satan fell from heaven in the beginning; by the just sentence of his Creator he fell, against whom he had rebelled. And when he had succeeded in gaining man to join him in his rebellion, and our Maker came to save men, then the brief hour of triumph came, and he made the most of it. When the Holiest had taken flesh, and was in his power, then in his revenge and malice he determined, as he himself had been struck down by the Almighty Arm, to strike in turn a heavy blow at Him who struck him. Therefore it was that Jesus fell down so suddenly. O dear Lord, by this Thy first fall raise us all out of sin, who have so miserably fallen under its power.

IV. HER PART

There is no part of the history of Jesus but Mary has her part in it. There are those who profess to be His servants, who think that her work was ended when she bore Him, and after that she had nothing to do but disappear and be forgotten. But we, O Lord, Thy children of the Catholic Church, do not so think of Thy Mother. She brought the tender infant into the

Temple, she lifted Him up in her arms when the wise men came to adore Him. She fled with Him to Egypt, she took Him up to Jerusalem when He was twelve years old. He lived with her at Nazareth for thirty years. She was with Him at the marriage-feast. Even when He had left her to preach, she hovered about Him. And now she shows herself as He toils along the Sacred Way with His cross on His shoulders. Sweet Mother, let us ever think of thee when we think of Jesus, and when we pray to Him, ever aid us by thy powerful intercession.

V. IN HIS WORK

Jesus could bear His cross alone, did He so will; but He permits Simon to help Him, in order to remind us that we must take part in His sufferings, and have a fellowship in His work. His merit is infinite, yet He condescends to let His people add their merit to it. The sanctity of the Blessed Virgin, the blood of the Martyrs, the prayers and penances of the saints, the good deeds of all the faithful, take part in that work which, nevertheless, is perfect without them. He saves us by His blood, but it is through and with ourselves that He saves us. Dear Lord, teach us to suffer with Thee, make it pleasant to us to suffer for Thy sake, and sanctify all our sufferings by the merits of Thy own.

VI. OUR HEARTS

Jesus let the pious woman carry off an impression of His Sacred Countenance, which was to last to future ages. He did this to remind us all, that His image must ever be impressed on all our hearts. Whoever we are, in whatever part of the earth, in whatever age of the world, Jesus must live in our hearts. We may differ from each other in many things, but in this we must all agree, if we are His true children. We must bear about with us the napkin of Saint Veronica; we must ever meditate upon His death and resurrection, we must ever imitate His divine excellence, according to our measure. Lord, let our countenances be ever pleasing in Thy sight, not defiled with sin, but bathed and washed white in Thy Precious Blood.

VII. WITH THEE

Satan had a second fall, when our Lord came upon earth. By that time he had usurped the dominion of the whole world—and he called himself its king. And he dared to take up the Holy Savior in his arms, and show Him all kingdoms, and blasphemously promise to give them to Him, his Maker, if He would adore him. Jesus answered, "Begone, Satan!"—and Satan fell down from the high mountain. And Jesus bore witness to it when He said, "I saw Satan, as lightning, falling from heaven." The Evil One remembered this second defeat, and so now he smote down the Innocent Lord a second time, now that he had Him in his power. O dear Lord, teach us to suffer with Thee, and not be afraid of Satan's buffetings when they come on us from resisting him.

VIII. AT THY OWN TIME

Ever since the prophecy of old time, that the Savior of man was to be born of a woman of the stock of Abraham, the Jewish women had desired to bear Him. Yet, now that He was really come, how different, as the Gospel tells us, was the event from what they had expected. He said to them "that the days were coming when they should say, 'blessed are the barren, and the wombs that have not borne, and the breasts which have not given suck.'" Ah, Lord, we know not what is good for us, and what is bad. We cannot foretell the future, nor do we know, when Thou comest to visit us, in what form Thou wilt come. And therefore we leave it all to Thee. Do Thou Thy good pleasure to us and in us. Let us ever look at Thee, and do Thou look upon us, and give us the grace of Thy bitter cross and passion, and console us in Thy own way and at Thy own time.

IX. THY AWFUL HUMILIATION

Satan will have a third and final fall at the end of the world, when he will be shut up for good in the everlasting fiery prison. He knew this was to be his end—he has no hope, but despair only. He knew that no suffering which he could at that moment inflict upon the Savior of men would avail to rescue himself from that inevitable doom. But, in horrible rage and hatred, he determined to insult and torture while he could the great King whose throne is everlasting.

Therefore, a third time he smote Him down fiercely to the earth. O Jesus, Only-begotten Son of God, the Word Incarnate, we adore with fear and trembling and deep thankfulness Thy awful humiliation, that Thou, who art the Highest, should have permitted Thyself, even for one hour, to be the sport and prey of the Evil One.

X. For Anything on Earth

Jesus would give up everything of this world, before He left it. He exercised the most perfect poverty. When He left the holy house of Nazareth, and went out to preach, He had not where to lay His head. He lived on the poorest food, and on what was given to Him by those who loved and served Him. And therefore He chose a death in which not even His clothes were left to Him. He parted with what seemed most necessary, and even a part of Him, by the law of human nature since the fall. Grant us in like manner, O dear Lord, to care nothing for anything on earth, and to bear the loss of all things, and to endure even shame, reproach, contempt, and mockery, rather than that Thou shalt be ashamed of us at the last day.

XI. Crucify Us with Thee

Jesus is pierced through each hand and each foot with a sharp nail. His eyes are dimmed with blood, and are closed by the swollen lids and livid brows which the blows of His executioners have caused.

His mouth is filled with vinegar and gall. His head is encircled by the sharp thorns. His heart is pierced with the spear. Thus, all His senses are mortified and crucified, that He may make atonement for every kind of human sin. O Jesus, mortify and crucify us with Thee. Let us never sin by hand or foot, by eyes or mouth, or by head or heart. Let all our senses be a sacrifice to Thee; let every member sing Thy praise. Let the sacred blood which flowed from Thy five wounds anoint us with such sanctifying grace that we may die to the world, and live only to Thee.

XII. THE DEATH OF HIS SON

"Consummatum est." It is completed—it has come to a full end. The mystery of God's love toward us is accomplished. The price is paid, and we are redeemed. The Eternal Father determined not to pardon us without a price, in order to show us especial favor. He condescended to make us valuable to Him. He might have saved us without a price—by the mere *fiat* of His will. But to show His love for us, He took a price, which, if there was to be a price set upon us at all, if there was any ransom at all to be taken for the guilt of our sins, could be nothing short of the death of His Son in our nature. O my God and Father, Thou hast valued us so much as to pay the highest of all possible prices for our sinful souls—and shall we not love and choose Thee above all things as the one necessary and one only good?

XIII. ONCE AGAIN

He is thy property now, O Virgin Mother, once again, for He and the world have met and parted. He went out from thee to do His Father's work—and He has done and suffered it. Satan and bad men have now no longer any claim upon Him—too long has He been in their arms. Satan took Him up aloft to the high mountain; evil men lifted Him up upon the cross. He has not been in thy arms, O Mother of God, since He was a child—but now thou hast a claim upon Him, when the world has done its worst. For thou art the all-favored, all-blessed, all-gracious Mother of the Highest. We rejoice in this great mystery. He has been hidden in thy womb, He has lain in thy bosom, He has been suckled at thy breasts, He has been carried in thy arms—and now that He is dead, He is placed upon thy lap. Virgin Mother of God, pray for us.

XIV. TO THYSELF

Jesus, when He was nearest to His everlasting triumph, seemed to be farthest from triumphing. When He was nearest upon entering upon His kingdom, and exercising all power in heaven and earth, He was lying dead in a cave of the rock. He was wrapped round in burying clothes, and confined within a sepulcher of stone, where He was soon to have a glorified spiritual body, which could penetrate all substances, go to and fro quicker than thought, and was about to ascend on high. Make us to trust in Thee, O Jesus, that Thou wilt display in us a similar providence. Make us sure, O Lord, that the greater is our distress, the nearer we are to Thee. The more men scorn us, the more Thou dost honor us. The more men insult us, the higher Thou wilt exalt us. The more they forget us, the more Thou dost keep us in mind. The more they abandon us, the closer Thou wilt bring us to Thyself.

LET US PRAY

God, who by the Precious Blood of Thy only-begotten Son didst sanctify the standard of the cross, grant we beseech Thee, that all those who rejoice in the glory of the same holy cross, may at all times and places rejoice in Thy protection, through the same Christ, our Lord.

RERUM CREATOR OPTIME

Who madest all and dost control,
    Lord, with Thy touch divine,
Cast out the slumbers of the soul,
    The rest that is not Thine.

Look down, Eternal Holiness,
    And wash the sins away,
Of those, who, rising to confess,
    Outstrip the lingering day.

Our hearts and hands by night, O Lord,
    We lift them in our need;
As holy Psalmists give the word,
    And holy Paul the deed.

Each sin to Thee of years gone by,
    Each hidden stain lies bare;
We shrink not from Thine awful eye,
    But pray that Thou wouldst spare.

Grant this, O Father, Only Son,
    And Spirit, God of grace,
To whom all worship shall be done
    In every time and place.

GAZE ON ME

But here I see One dropping blood, gashed by the thong, and stretched upon the Cross, and He is God. It is no tale of human woe which I am reading here; it is the record of the passion of the great Creator. The Word and Wisdom of the Father, who dwelt in His bosom in bliss ineffable from eternity, whose very smile has shed radiance and grace over the whole creation, whose traces I see in the starry heavens and on the green earth, this glorious living God, it is He who looks at me so piteously, so tenderly from the Cross. He seems to say,—I cannot move, though I am omnipotent, for sin hath bound Me here. I had it in mind to come on earth among innocent creatures, more fair and lovely than them all, with a face more radiant than the Seraphim, and a form as royal as that of Archangels, to be their equal yet their God, to fill them with My grace, to receive their worship, to enjoy their company, and to prepare them for the heaven to which I destined them; but, before I carried My purpose into effect, they sinned, and lost their inheritance; and so I come indeed, but come, not in the brightness in which I went forth to create the morning stars and to fill the sons of God with melody, but in deformity and in shame, in sighs and tears, with blood upon My cheek, and with My limbs bare and rent. Gaze on Me, O My children, if you will, for I am helpless; gaze on your Maker, in faith and love. Here I wait upon the Cross, the appointed time of grace and mercy; here I wait till the end of the world, silent and motionless, for the conversion of the sinful and the consolation of the just; here I remain in weakness and in shame, though I am so great in heaven till the end, patiently expecting My full catalog of souls, when time is at length over, shall be the reward of My passion and the triumph of My grace to all eternity. . . .

Our Lord's sufferings were so great, because His soul was in suffering. What shows this is that His soul began to suffer before His bodily passion, as we see in the agony in the garden. The first anguish which came upon His body was not from without—it was not from the scourges, the thorns, or the nails, but from His soul. His soul was in such agony that He called it death: "My soul is sorrowful even unto death." The anguish was such that it, as it were, burst open His whole body. It was a pang affecting His heart; as in the deluge the floods of the great deep were broken up and the windows of heaven were open. The blood, rushing from His tormented heart, forced its way on every side, formed for itself a thousand new channels, filled all the pores, and at length stood forth upon His skin in thick drops, which fell heavily on the ground.

He remained in this living death from the time of His agony in the garden; and as His first agony was from His soul, so was His last. As the scourge and the cross did not begin His sufferings, so they did not close them. It was the agony of His soul, not of His body, which caused His death. His persecutors were surprised to hear that He was dead. How, then, did He die? That agonized, tormented heart, which at the beginning so awfully relieved itself in the rush of blood and the bursting of His pores, at length broke. It broke and He died. It would have broken *at once*, had He not kept it from breaking. At length the moment came. He gave the word and His heart broke. . . .

O my God and Savior, who wentest through sufferings for me with such lively consciousness, such precision, such recollection, and such fortitude, enable me, by Thy help, if I am brought into the power of this terrible trial, bodily pain, enable me to bear it with some portion of Thy calmness. Obtain for me this grace, O Virgin Mother, who didst see thy Son suffer and didst suffer with Him; that I, when I suffer, may associate my sufferings with His and with thine, and that through His passion, and thy merits, and those of all saints, they may be a satisfaction for my sins and procure for me eternal life.

Jesu, Master! when we sin,
    Turn on us Thy healing face;
It will melt the offence within
    Into penitential grace:

Beam on our bewilder'd mind,
    Till its dreamy shadows flee;
Stones cry out where Thou hast shined,
    Jesu! musical with Thee.
To the Father and the Son,
    And the Spirit, Who in Heaven
Ever witness, Three and One,
    Praise on Earth be ever given.

The Power of the Cross

O my great God, Thou hast humbled Thyself, Thou hast stooped to take our flesh and blood, and hast been lifted up upon the tree! I praise and glorify Thee tenfold the more, because Thou hast shown Thy power by means of Thy suffering, than hadst Thou carried on Thy work without it. It is worthy of Thy infinitude thus to surpass and transcend all our thoughts.

In Spite of the World

Lord Jesu, I believe, and by Thy grace will ever believe and hold, and I know that it is true, and will be true to the end of the world, that nothing great is done without suffering, without humiliation, and that all things are possible by means of it. I believe, O my God, that poverty is better than riches, pain better than pleasure, obscurity and contempt than fame, and ignominy and reproach than honor. My Lord, I do not ask Thee to bring these trials on me, for I know not if I could face them; but at least, O Lord, whether I be in prosperity or adversity, I will believe that it is as I have said. I will never have faith in riches, rank, power, or reputation. I will never set my heart on worldly success or on worldly advantages. I will ever, with Thy grace, make much of those who are despised or neglected, honor the poor, revere the suffering, and admire and venerate Thy saints and confessors, and take my part with them in spite of the world. Amen.

THE PROMISE

And lastly, O my dear Lord, though I am so very weak that I am not fit to ask Thee for suffering as a gift, and have not strength to do so, at least I will beg of Thee grace to meet suffering well, when Thou in Thy love and wisdom dost bring it upon me, knowing that in this way I shall gain the promise both of this life and of the next. Amen.

A MATERIAL BODY

I adore Thee, O Eternal Word, for Thy gracious condescension, in not only taking a created nature, a created spirit or soul, but a material body. I adore Thy most holy Body, O my dear Jesus, the instrument of our redemption!

BEAUTIFUL AND GLORIOUS

I look at Thee, my Lord Jesus, and think of Thy most holy Body, and I keep it before me as the pledge of my own resurrection. Though I die, as die I certainly shall, nevertheless I shall not forever die, for I shall rise again. O Thou who art the Truth, I know, and believe with my whole heart, that this very flesh of mine will rise again. I know, base and odious as it is at present, that it will one day, if I be worthy, be raised incorruptible and altogether beautiful and glorious. This I know; this, by Thy grace, I will ever keep before me. Amen.

THE SIGN

Thou art more beautiful in Thy weakness than in Thy strength; Thy wounds shine like stars of light; Thy very Cross becomes an object of worship; the instruments of Thy Passion, the nails and the thorny crown, are replete with miraculous power. So Thou bidest the commemoration of Thy Bloody Sacrifice to be made day by day all over the earth, and Thou Thyself art there in Person to quicken and sanctify it; Thou doest rear Thy saving Cross in every Church and over every Altar; Thou showest Thyself torn and bleeding upon the wood at the corners of each street and in every village marketplace; Thou makest it the symbol of Thy religion; Thou sealest our foreheads, our lips, and our breast with this triumphant sign; with it Thou beginest and endest our days, and with it Thou consignest us to the tomb. And when Thou comest again, that Sign of the Son of Man will be seen in Heaven; and when Thou takest Thy seat in judgment, the same glorious marks will be seen by all the world in Thy Hands, Feet, and Side, which were dug into them at the season of Thy degradation. . . .

O Lord Jesus Christ, who, when Thou wast about to suffer, didst pray for Thy disciples to the end of time that they might all be one, as Thou art in the Father, and the Father in Thee, look down in pity on the manifold divisions among those who profess Thy faith, and heal the many wounds which the pride of man and the craft of Satan have inflicted upon Thy people. Thou art chosen to be His, even above thy fellows who dwell in the East and South. What a thought is this, a thought almost too great for our understanding! . . .

Set free the prisoners from unauthorised forms of worship, and bring them all into the One Holy Catholic and Apostolic Church. Teach all men that the See of Saint Peter, the Holy Church of Rome, is the foundation, center, and instrument of unity. Open their hearts to the long-forgotten truth that our Holy Father, the Pope, is Thy Vicar and Representative; and that in obeying him in matters of religion, they are obeying Thee, so that as there is but one holy company in heaven above, so likewise there may be but one communion, confessing and glorifying Thy holy Name here below. Amen.

"Come to Me"

"His eyes were a flame of fire," and "His countenance shone as the sun shineth in his strength."

O my God, the day will come when I shall see that countenance and those eyes, when my soul returns to Him to be judged.

Those eyes are so piercing; they see through me; nothing is hid from them. Thou countest every hair of my head; Thou knowest every breath I breathe; Thou seest every morsel of food I take.

Those eyes are so pure. They are so clear that I can look into their depths, as into some transparent well of water, though I cannot see the bottom; for Thou art infinite.

Those eyes are so loving; so gentle, so sweet; they seem to say, "come to me." . . .

All Thy providences, all Thy dealings with us, all Thy judgments, mercies, warnings, deliverances, tend to peace and repose as their ultimate issue. All our troubles and pleasures here, all our anxieties, fears, doubts, difficulties, hopes, encouragements, afflictions, losses, attainments, tend this one way. After Christmas, Easter, Whitsuntide, comes Trinity Sunday, and the weeks that follow; and in like manner, after our soul's anxious travail; after the birth of the Spirit; after trial and temptation; after sorrow and pain; after daily dyings to the world; after daily risings unto holiness; at length comes that "rest which remaineth unto the people of God." After the fever of life; after weariness and sicknesses; fightings and despondings; languor and fretfulness; struggling and failing; struggling and succeeding; after all the changes and chances of this troubled unhealthy state, at length comes death, at length the White Throne of God, at length the Beatific Vision.

Grant this, O Father, Only Son,
    And Spirit, God of grace,
To whom all worship shall be done
    In every time and place.

STAY

I adore Thee, O my God, as the true and only Light! From Eternity to Eternity, before any creature was, when Thou wast alone, alone but not solitary, for Thou hast ever been Three in One, Thou wast the Infinite Light. There was none to see Thee but Thyself. Bright as are the angels, they are poor and most unworthy shadows of Thee. They are pale and look dim and gather blackness before Thee. They are so feeble beside Thee, that they are unable to gaze upon Thee. The highest Seraphim veil their eyes, by deed as well as by word proclaiming Thy unutterable glory. For me, I cannot even look upon the sun, and what is this but a base material emblem of Thee? How should I endure to look even on an angel? and how could I look upon Thee and live? If I were placed in the illumination of Thy countenance,

I should shrink up like the grass. O most gracious God, who shall approach Thee, being so glorious, yet how can I keep from Thee? Thou comest and goest at Thy will, O my God, I cannot keep Thee! I can only beg of Thee to stay. Remain till morning, and then go not without giving me a blessing. Remain with me till death in this dark valley, when the darkness will end. Remain, O Light of my soul. Shine on me, "O fire ever burning and never failing"—and I shall begin, through and in Thy Light, to see Light, and to recognise Thee truly, as the Source of Light. Stay, sweet Jesus, stay for ever. Amen.

VERBUM SUPERNUM PRODIENS

Supernal Word, proceeding from
    The Eternal Father's breast,
And in the end of ages come,
    To aid a world distrest;

Enlighten, Lord, and set on fire
    Our spirits with Thy love,
That, dead to earth, they may aspire
    And live to joys above.

That, when the judgment-seat on high
    Shall fix the sinner's doom,
And to the just a glad voice cry,
    Come to your destined home;

Safe from the black and yawning lake
    Of restless, endless pain,

We may the face of God partake,
    The bliss of heaven attain.

To God the Father, God the Son,
    And Holy Ghost, to Thee,
As heretofore, when time is done,
    Unending glory be.

WHEN MARY GAZED ON HIM

Think you not that to Mary, when she held Him in her maternal arms, when she gazed on the pale countenance and the dislocated limbs of her God, when she traced the wandering lines of blood, when she counted the weals, the bruises, and the wounds, which dishonored that virginal flesh, think you not that to her eyes it was the more beautiful than when she first worshiped it, pure, and radiant, and fragrant, on the night of His nativity? . . . Thy glory sullied, Thy beauty marred, those five wounds welling blood, those temples torn and raw, that broken heart, that crushed and livid frame, they teach me more than were Thou Solomon "in the diadem wherewith his mother crowned him in the day of his heart's joy." The gentle and tender expression of that Countenance is no new beauty, or created grace; it is but the manifestation, in a human form, of attributes which have been from everlasting. Thou canst not change, O Jesus; and, as Thou art still Mystery, so wast Thou always Love. I cannot comprehend Thee more than I did, before I saw Thee on the cross; but I have gained my lesson. I have before me the proof, that in spite of Thy awful nature, and the clouds and darkness which surround it, Thou canst think of me with a personal affection. Thou hast died, that I might live. "Let us love God," says Thy Apostle, "because He first hath loved us." I can love Thee now from first to last, though from first to last I cannot understand Thee. As I adore Thee, O Lover of souls, in Thy humiliation, so will I admire Thee and embrace Thee in Thy infinite and everlasting power.

THY GRACE

O my God, suffer me still—bear with me in spite of my waywardness, perverseness, and ingratitude! I improve very slowly, but really I am moving on to heaven, or at least I wish to move. Only give me Thy grace—meet me with Thy grace, I will through Thy grace do what I can—and Thou shalt perfect it for me. Then I shall have happy days in Thy presence, and in the sight and adoration of Thy five Sacred Wounds.

RERUM DEUS TENAX VIGOR

O God, unchangeable and true,
    Of all the Life and Power,
Dispensing light in silence through
    Every successive hour,

Lord, brighten our declining day,
    That it may never wane,
Till death, when all things round decay,
    Brings back the morn again.

This grace on Thy redeem'd confer,
  Father, Co-equal Son,
And Holy Ghost, the Comforter,
  Eternal Three in One.

A WANT IN MY NATURE

It is a want in my nature to have one who can weep with me, and rejoice with me, and in a way minister to me; and this would be presumption in me, and worse, to hope to find in the Infinite and Eternal God. This is what you may be tempted to say, my brethren. . . . Never suppose that you are left by God; never suppose that He does not know you, your minds and your powers, better than you do yourselves. . . .

O mysteries, that the ineffable love of Father to Son should be the love of the Son to us! Why was it, O Lord? What good thing didst Thou see in me a sinner? Why wast Thou set on me? "What is man, that Thou art mindful of him?" This poor flesh of mine, this weak sinful soul, which has no life except in Thy grace, Thou didst set Thy love upon it. Complete Thy work, O Lord, and as Thou hast loved me from the beginning, so make me to love Thee unto the end. . . .

Make me like Thyself, O my God, since in spite of myself, such Thou canst make me. Thou hast shown it to be possible in the face of the whole world by the most overwhelming proof, by taking our created nature on Thyself and exalting it to Thee. Let me be partaker of that Divine Nature in all the riches of Its attributes, which in fullness of substance and in personal presence became the Son of Mary.

The Sacred Heart

O Sacred Heart of Jesus, I adore Thee in the oneness of the Personality of the Second Person of the Holy Trinity. Whatever belongs to the Person of Jesus, belongs therefore to God, and is to be worshiped with that one and the same worship which we pay to Jesus. He did not take on Him His human nature, as something distinct and separate from Himself, but as simply, absolutely, eternally His, so as to be included by us in the very thought of Him. I worship Thee, O Heart of Jesus, as being Jesus Himself, as being that Eternal Word in human nature which He took wholly and lives in wholly, and therefore in Thee. Thou art the Heart of the Most High made man. I worship Thee, as bearing a part in that passion which is my life, for Thou didst burst and break, through agony, in the garden of Gethsemani, and Thy precious contents trickled out, through the veins and pores of the skin, upon the earth. And again, Thou hadst been drained all but dry upon the cross; and then, after death, Thou wast pierced by the lance, and gavest out the small remains of that inestimable treasure, which is our redemption.

Lux Ecce Surgit Aurea

See, the golden dawn is glowing,
While the paly shades are going,

Which have led us far and long,
In a labyrinth of wrong.

May it bring us peace serene;
May it cleanse, as it is clean;
Plain and clear our words be spoke,
And our thoughts without a cloak;

So the day's account shall stand.
Guileless tongue and holy hand,
Stedfast eyes and unbeguiled,
"Flesh as of a little child."

There is One Who from above
Watches how the still hours move
Of our day of service done,
From the dawn to setting sun.

To the Father, and the Son,
And the Spirit, Three and One,
As of old, and as in Heaven,
Now and here be glory given.

—III.—

RISEN SAVIOR

Millions of souls are conversing
with Him, are venturing at His word,
are looking for His presence.

Nox et Tenebrae et Nubila

Haunting gloom and flitting shades,
    Ghastly shapes, away!
Christ is rising, and pervades
    Highest Heaven with day.

He with His bright spear the night
    Dazzles and pursues;
Earth wakes up, and glows with light
    Of a thousand hues.

Thee, O Christ, and Thee alone,
    With a single mind,
We with chant and plaint would own:
    To Thy flock be kind.

Much it needs Thy light divine,
    Spot and stain to clean;
Light of Angels, on us shine
    With Thy face serene.

To the Father, and the Son,
    And the Holy Ghost,
Here be glory, as is done
    By the angelic host.

One Name That Lives

There is just one Name in the whole world that
lives; it is the Name of One who passed His years in

obscurity, and who died a malefactor's death. Eighteen hundred years have gone by since that time, but still it has its hold upon the human mind. It has possessed the world, and it maintains possession. Amid the most various nations, under the most diversified circumstances, in the most cultivated, in the rudest races and intellects, in all classes of society, the Owner of that great Name reigns. High and low, rich and poor, acknowledge Him. Millions of souls are conversing with Him, are venturing at His word, are looking for His presence. Palaces sumptuous, innumerable, are raised to His honor; His image, in its deepest humiliations, is triumphantly displayed in the proud city, in the open country, at the corners of streets, on the tops of mountains. It sanctifies the ancestral hall, the closet, and the bedchamber; it is the subject for the exercise of the highest genius in the imitative arts. It is worn next to the heart in life; it is held before the failing eyes in death. Here, then, is One who is not a mere name; He is no empty fiction, He is a substance; He is dead and gone, but still He lives—as the living, energetic thought of successive generations, and as the awful motive power of a thousand great events.

SPLENDOR PATERNAE GLORIAE

Of the Father Effluence bright,
Out of Light evolving light,

Light from Light, unfailing Ray,
Day creative of the day:
Truest Sun, upon us stream
With Thy calm perpetual beam,
In the Spirit's still sunshine
Making sense and thought divine.

Seek we too the Father's face,
Father of almighty grace,
And of majesty excelling,
Who can purge our tainted dwelling;

Who can aid us, who can break
Teeth of envious foes, and make
Hours of loss and pain succeed,
Guiding safe each duteous deed,

And infusing self-control,
Fragrant chastity of soul,
Faith's keen flame to soar on high,
Incorrupt simplicity.

Christ Himself for food be given,
Faith become the cup of Heaven,
Out of which the joy is quaff'd
Of the Spirit's sobering draught.

With that joy replenished,
Morn shall glow with modest red,
Noon with beaming faith be bright,
Eve be soft without twilight.

It has dawn'd;—upon our way,
Father in Thy Word, this day,
In Thy Father Word Divine,
From Thy cloudy pillar shine.

To the Father, and the Son,
And the Spirit, Three and One,
As of old, and as in Heaven,
Now and here be glory given.

CHRIST IN HIS HOLY CHURCH

O blessed day of the Resurrection, which of old time was called the queen of Festivals, and raised among Christians an anxious, nay contentious diligence duly to honor it! Blessed day, once only passed in sorrow, when the Lord actually rose, and the Disciples believed not; but ever since a day of joy to the faith and love of the Church! In ancient times, Christians all over the world began it with a morning salutation. Each man said to his neighbor, "Christ is risen"; and his neighbor answered him, "Christ is risen indeed, and hath appeared to Simon!" To Simon Peter, the favored Apostle on whom the Church is built, Christ has appeared. He has appeared to His Holy Church first of all, and in the Church He dispenses blessings, such as the world knows not of. Blessed are they if they knew their blessedness, who are allowed, as we are, week after week, and Festival after Festival, to seek and find in that Holy Church the Savior of their souls!

Lucis Creator Optime

Father of Lights, by whom each day
    Is kindled out of night,
Who, when the heavens were made, didst lay
    Their rudiments in light;

Thou who didst bind and blend in one
    The glistening morn and evening pale,
Hear Thou our plaint, when light is gone,
    And lawlessness and strife prevail.

Hear, lest the whelming weight of crime
    Wreck us with life in view;
Lest thoughts and schemes of sense and time
    Earn us a sinner's due.

So may we knock at Heaven's door,
    And strive the immortal prize to win,
Continually and evermore
    Guarded without and pure within.

Grant this, O Father, Only Son,
    And Spirit, God of grace,
To whom all worship shall be done
    In every time and place.

Of Heaven

My God, let me never forget that seasons of consolation are refreshments here, and nothing more; not our abiding state. They will not remain with us, ex-

cept in heaven. Here they are only intended to prepare us for doing and suffering. I pray Thee, O my
God, to give them to me from time to time. Shed over
me the sweetness of Thy Presence, lest I faint by the
way; lest I find religious service wearisome, through
my exceeding infirmity, and give over prayer. Give me
Thy Divine consolations from time to time; but let me
not rest in them. Let me use them for the purpose for
which Thou givest them. Let me not think it grievous,
let me not be downcast, if they go. Let them carry me
forward to the thought and the desire of heaven.

FORBEARANCE OF JESUS

I adore Thee, O my Lord, for Thy wonderful patience
and Thy compassionate tender-hearted condescension. Thy disciples, in spite of all Thy teaching and
miracles, disbelieved Thee when they saw Thee die,
and fled. Nor did they take courage afterwards, nor
think of Thy promise of rising again on the third
day. They did not believe Magdalen, nor the other
women, who said they had seen Thee alive again. Yet
Thou didst appear to them—Thou didst show them
Thy wounds—Thou didst let them touch Thee—Thou
didst eat before them, and give them Thy peace. O
Jesu, is any obstinacy too great for Thy love? Thou
dost forgive not only seven times, but to seventy
times seven. Many waters cannot quench a love like
Thine. And such Thou art all over the earth, even
to the end—forgiving, sparing, forbearing, waiting,
though sinners are ever provoking Thee; pitying and

taking into account their ignorance, visiting all men, all Thine enemies, with the gentle pleadings of Thy grace, day after day, year after year, up to the hour of their death—for He knoweth whereof we are made; He knoweth we are but dust.

"It Is I; Be Not Afraid"

When I sink down in gloom or fear,
    Hope blighted or delay'd,
Thy whisper, Lord, my heart shall cheer,
    "'Tis I; be not afraid!"

Or, startled at some sudden blow,
    If fretful thoughts I feel,
"Fear not, it is but I!" shall flow,
    As balm my wound to heal.

Nor will I quit Thy way, though foes
    Some onward pass defend;
From each rough voice the watchword goes,
    "Be not afraid! . . . a friend!"

And oh! when judgment's trumpet clear
    Awakes me from the grave,
Still in its echo may I hear,
    "'Tis Christ; He comes to save."

Parting with His Apostles

I adore Thee, O my God! together with Thy Apostles, during the forty days in which Thou didst visit them after Thy resurrection. So blessed was the time, so calm, so undisturbed from without, that it was good to be there with Thee, and when it was over, they could hardly believe that it was more than begun. How quickly must that first Paschal Time have flown! and they perhaps hardly knew when it was to end. O what a time of consolation! What a contrast to what had lately taken place! It was their happy time on earth—the foretaste of heaven; not noticed, not interfered with, by man. They passed it in wonder, in musing, in adoration, rejoicing in Thy light, O my risen God!

THOU KNEWEST WELL

But Thou, O my dear Lord, didst know better than they! They hoped and desired, perhaps fancied, that that resting time, that *refrigerium,* never would end till it was superseded by something better; but Thou didst know, in Thy eternal wisdom, that, in order to arrive at what was higher than any blessing which they were then enjoying, it was fitting, it was necessary that they should sustain conflict and suffering. Thou knewest well, that unless Thou hadst departed, the Paraclete could not have come to them; and therefore Thou didst go, that they might gain more by Thy sorrowful absence than by Thy sensible visitations. I adore Thee, O Father, for sending the Son and the Holy Ghost! I adore Thee, O Son, and Thee, O Holy Ghost, for vouchsafing to be sent to us!

Te Lucis Ante Terminum

Now that the daylight dies away,
    By all Thy grace and love,
Thee, Maker of the world, we pray
    To watch our bed above.

Let dreams depart and phantoms fly,
    The offspring of the night,
Keep us, like shrines, beneath Thine eye,
    Pure in our foe's despite.

This grace on Thy redeem'd confer,
    Father, Co-equal Son,
And Holy Ghost, the Comforter,
    Eternal Three in One.

O Memorable Day!

My Lord, I follow Thee up to heaven; as Thou goest up, my heart and mind go with Thee. Never was triumph like this. Thou didst appear a babe in human flesh at Bethlehem. That flesh, taken from the Blessed Virgin, was not before Thou didst form it into a body; it was a new work of Thy hands. And Thy soul was new altogether, created by Thy Omnipotence, at the moment when Thou didst enter into her sacred breast. That pure soul and body, taken as a garment for Thyself, began on earth, and never had been elsewhere. This is the triumph. Earth rises to heaven. I see that Form which hung upon the cross, those scarred hands and feet, that pierced side; they are mounting up to heaven. And the angels are full of jubilee; the myriads of blessed spirits, which people the glorious expanse, part like the waters to let Thee pass. And the living pavement of God's palaces is cleft in twain, and the Cherubim with flaming swords, who form the rampart of heaven against fallen man, give way and open out, that Thou mayest enter, and Thy saints after Thee. O memorable day!

EMMANUEL ENTERS HEAVEN

O memorable day! The Apostles feel it to be so, now that it is come, though they felt so differently before it came. When it was coming they dreaded it. They could not think but it would be a great bereavement; but now, as we read, they returned to Jerusalem "with great joy." Oh, what a time of triumph! They understood it now. They understood how weak it had been in them to grudge their Lord and Master, the glorious Captain of their salvation, the Champion and First Fruits of the human family, this crown of His great work. It was the triumph of redeemed man. It is the completion of his redemption. It was the last act, making the whole sure, for now man is actually in heaven. The sinful race has now one of its own children there, its own flesh and blood, in the person of the Eternal Son. Oh, what a wonderful marriage between heaven and earth! It began in sorrow; but now the long travail of that mysterious wedding day is over; the marriage feast is begun;

marriage and birth have gone together; man is new born when Emmanuel enters heaven.

CREATOR ALME SIDERUM

Creator of the starry pole,
  Savior of all who live,
And light of every faithful soul,
  Jesu, these prayers receive.

Who sooner than our foe malign
  Should triumph, from above
Didst come, to be the medicine
  Of a sick world, in love;

And the deep wounds to cleanse and cure
  Of a whole race, didst go,
Pure Victim, from a Virgin pure,
  The bitter cross unto.

Who hast a Name, and hast a Power,
  The height and depth to sway,
And angels bow, and devils cower,
  In transport or dismay;

Thou too shalt be our Judge at length;
  Lord, in Thy grace bestow
Thy weapons of celestial strength,
  And snatch us from the foe.

Honor and glory, power and praise,
  To Father, and to Son,

And Holy Ghost, be paid always,
    The Eternal Three in One.

THE WAY

My Lord Jesu, I confess and know that Thou only art the True, the Beautiful, and the Good. Thou alone canst make me bright and glorious, and canst lead me up after Thee. Thou art the Way, the Truth, and the Life, and none but Thou. Earth will never lead me to Heaven. Thou alone art the Way; Thou alone.

TO THEE

My God, shall I for one moment doubt where my path lies? Shall I not at once take Thee for my portion? To whom should I go? Thou hast the words of eternal Life. Thou camest down for the very purpose of doing that which no one here below could do for me. None but He who is in heaven can bring me to heaven. Though I served the world ever so well, though I did my duty in it (as men speak), what could the world do for me, however hard it tried? Though I filled my station well, did good to my fellows, had a fair name or a wide reputation, though I did great deeds and was celebrated, though I had the praise of history, how would all this bring me to heaven? I choose Thee then for my One Portion, because Thou livest and diest not. I cast away all idols. I give myself to *Thee*. I pray Thee to teach me, guide me, enable me, and receive me to Thee.

Ever Waiting

Thou hast surrounded me from childhood with Thy mercies; Thou hast taken as much pains with me as if I was of importance to Thee, and my loss of heaven would be Thy loss of me. Thou hast led me on by ten thousand merciful providences; Thou hast brought me near to Thee in the most intimate of ways; Thou hast brought me into Thy house and chamber; Thou hast fed me with Thyself. Dost Thou not love me?—really, truly, substantially, efficaciously love me, without any limitation of the word? I know it. I have an utter conviction of it. Thou art ever waiting to do me benefits, to pour upon me blessings. Thou art ever waiting for me to ask Thee to be merciful to me.

Ever Listening

Yes, my Lord, Thou dost desire that I should ask Thee; Thou art ever listening for my voice. There is nothing I cannot get from Thee. Oh I confess my heinous neglect of this great privilege. I am very guilty. I have trifled with the highest of gifts, the power to move Omnipotence. How slack am I in praying to Thee for my own needs! how little have I thought of the needs of others! How little have I brought before Thee the needs of the world—of Thy Church! How little have I asked for graces in detail! and for aid in daily wants! How little have I interceded for individuals! How little have I accompanied actions and undertakings, in themselves good, with prayer for Thy guidance and blessing!

GOD ALONE

I adore Thee, O My God, with Thomas; and if I have, like him, sinned through unbelief, I adore Thee the more. "My God and my all." To have Thee is to have everything I can have. O my Eternal Father, give me Thyself. It would have been presumption, unless Thou hadst encouraged me. Thou hast put it into my mouth, Thou hast clothed Thyself in my nature, Thou hast become my Brother, Thou hast died as other men die, only in far greater bitterness, that, instead of my eyeing Thee fearfully from afar, I might confidently draw near to Thee. Thou dost beckon me to take hold of Thee. My God and my all, what could I say more than this, if I spoke to all eternity! I am full and abound and overflow, when I have Thee; but without Thee I am nothing—I wither away, I dissolve and perish. My Lord and my God, my God and my all, give me Thyself and nothing else.

TO BEAR THY PRESENCE

Thomas came and touched Thy sacred wounds. O will the day ever come when I shall be allowed actually and visibly to kiss them? What a day will that be when I am thoroughly cleansed from all impurity and sin, and am fit to draw near to my Incarnate God in His palace of light above! what a morning, when having done with all penal suffering, I see Thee for the first time with these very eyes of mine, I see Thy countenance, gaze upon Thy eyes and gracious lips without quailing, and then kneel down with joy to kiss Thy feet, and am welcomed into Thy arms. What a day, a long day without ending, the day of eternity, when I shall be so unlike what I am *now*, when I feel in myself a body of death, and am perplexed and distracted with ten thousand thoughts. O my Lord, what a day when I shall have done once for all with all sins, venial as well as mortal, and shall stand perfect and acceptable in Thy sight, able to bear Thy presence, nothing shrinking from Thy eye, not shrinking from the pure scrutiny of Angels and Archangels, when I stand in their midst and they around me!

To Surrender Myself

O my God, though I am not fit to see or touch Thee yet, still I will ever come within Thy reach, and desire that which is not yet given me in its fulness. O my Savior, Thou shalt be my sole God!—I will have no Lord but Thee. I will break to pieces all idols in my heart which rival Thee. I will have nothing but Jesus and Him crucified. It shall be my life to pray to Thee, to offer myself to Thee, to keep Thee before me, to worship Thee in Thy holy Sacrifice, and to surrender myself to Thee in Holy Communion.

Unconquerable Love

My God, what hast Thou done for me! I fall, yet Thou dost not cast me off. In spite of all my sins, Thou dost still love me, prosper me, comfort me, surround me with blessings, sustain me and further me. Thou art as kind as if I had nothing to explain, to repent of, to amend—as if I were Thy best, most faithful, most steady and loyal friend. Nay, alas! I am even led to presume upon Thy love. Every day is but a fresh memorial of Thy unwearied, unconquerable love!

Our Home

O how great a good it will be . . . if the time shall one day come, when we shall enter into His tabernacle above, and hide ourselves under the shadow of His wings; if we shall be in the number of those blessed dead who die in the Lord, and rest from their labor. Here we are tossing upon the sea, and the wind is contrary. All through the day we are tried and tempted in various ways. We cannot think, speak, act, but infirmity and sin are at hand. But in the unseen world, where Christ has entered, all is peace. . . . "There is no more death, neither sorrow nor crying, neither any more pain; for the former things are passed away." Nor any more sin; nor any more guilt; no more remorse; no more punishment; no more penitence; no more trial; no more infirmity to depress us; no affection to mislead us; no passion to transport us; no prejudice to blind us; no sloth, no pride, no envy, no strife; but the light of God's countenance, and a pure river of water of life, clear as crystal proceeding out of the Throne. That is our home; here we are but on pilgrimage, and Christ is calling us home.

More Than Earthly

At times we seem to catch a glimpse of a Form which we shall hereafter see face to face. We approach, and in spite of the darkness, our hands, our head, our brow, or our lips become, as it were, sensible of the contact of something more than earthly. We know not where we are, but we have been bathing in water, and a voice tells us that it is blood. Or we have a mark signed upon our foreheads, and it spake of Calvary. Or we recollect a hand laid upon our heads, and surely it had the print of nails in it, and resembled His who with a touch gave sight to the blind and raised the dead. Or we have been eating and drinking; and it was not a dream surely, that One fed us from His wounded side, and renewed our nature by the heavenly meat He gave.

Without Thee

Now then give me this further grace, Lord, to use all this grace well, and to turn it to my salvation. Teach me, make me, to come to the fountains of mercy continually with an awakened, eager mind, and with lively devotion. Give me a love of Thy sacraments and ordinances. Teach me to value as I ought to prize as the inestimable pearl, that pardon which again and again Thou givest me, and the great and heavenly gift of the Presence of Him whose Spirit Thou art, upon the altar. Without Thee I can do nothing, and Thou art there where Thy Church is and Thy sacraments. Give me grace to rest in them forever, till they are lost in the glory of Thy manifestation in the world to come.

ALL OUR HOPES FOR THE FUTURE

"The Word was made flesh, and dwelt among us;" this is the glorious, unsearchable, incomprehensible truth, on which all our hopes for the future depend. . . . It is the wonderful economy of Redemption, by which God became man, the Highest became the lowest, the Creator took His place among His own creatures, Power became weakness, and Wisdom looked to men like folly. He that was rich was made poor; the Lord of all was rejected: "He came unto His own, and His own received Him not." . . . God in His mercy rouse my sluggish spirits, and inflame my earthly heart, that I may cease to be an exception in His great family, which is ever adoring, praising, and loving Him. . . .

We are slow to master the great truth, that Christ is, as it were, walking among us, and by His hand, or eye, or voice, bidding us follow Him. We do not understand that His call is a thing which takes place now. We think it took place in the Apostles' days; but we do not believe in it, we do not look out for it in our own case. We have not eyes to see the Lord; far different from the beloved Apostle, who knew Christ even when the rest of the disciples knew Him not. When He stood on the shore after His Resurrection, and bade them cast the net into the sea, "that disciple whom Jesus loved saith unto Peter, It is the Lord." . . .

O my God, Thou dost over-abound in mercy! To live by faith is my necessity, from my present state of being and from my sin; but Thou hast pronounced a blessing on it. Thou hast said that I am more blessed if I believe in Thee, than if I saw Thee.

MY BLESSEDNESS

My great God, Thou knowest all that is in the universe, because Thou Thyself didst make it. It is the very work of Thy hands. Thou are omniscient, because Thou art omni-creative. Thou knowest each part, however minute, as perfectly as Thou knowest the whole. Thou knowest mind as perfectly as Thou knowest matter. Thou knowest the thoughts and purposes of every soul as perfectly as if there were no other soul in the whole of Thy creation. Thou knowest me through and through; all my present, past, and future are before Thee as one whole. . . .

It was Thy supreme blessedness in the eternity past, as it is Thy blessedness in all eternities, to know Thyself, as Thou alone canst know Thee. O my God, what am I that Thou shouldst make my blessedness to consist in that which is Thy own! That Thou shouldst grant me to have not only the sight of Thee, but to share in Thy very own joy! . . .

At the end of millions of years I shall find in Thee, the same, or rather, greater sweetness than at first, and shall seem then only to be beginning to enjoy Thee; and so on for eternity I shall ever be a little child beginning to be taught the rudiments of Thy Infinite Divine Nature.

Be Merciful, Be Gracious

Be merciful, be gracious; Lord, deliver me.
From the sins that are past;
From Thy frown and Thine ire;
From the perils of dying;
From any complying
With sin or denying
My God, or relying
On self, at the last;
From the nethermost fire;
From all that is evil;
From the power of the devil;
Thy servant deliver;
For once and forever.
By Thy birth, and by Thy Cross,
Rescue me from endless loss;
By Thy death and burial,
Save me from a final fall;
By Thy rising from the tomb,
By Thy mounting up above,
By the Spirit's gracious love,
Save me in the day of doom.

— IV. —

HOLY GHOST

I adore Thee, My Lord and God, the Eternal
Paraclete, co-equal with the Father and Son.
I adore Thee as the Life of all that live.

Nunc Sancte Nobis Spiritus

Come, Holy Ghost, who ever One
Reignest with Father and with Son,
It is the hour, our souls possess
With Thy full flood of holiness.

Let flesh, and heart, and lips, and mind,
Sound forth our witness to mankind;
And love light up our mortal frame,
Till others catch the living flame.

Now to the Father, to the Son,
And to the Spirit, Three in One,
Be praise and thanks and glory given
By men on earth, by Saints in heaven.

The Paraclete

Lord Jesus, Thou didst not stay with Thy Apostles, as in the days of Thy flesh, but Thou didst come to them and abide with them forever, with a much more immediate and true communion in the power of the Paraclete. . . .

I adore Thee, My Lord and God, the Eternal Paraclete, co-equal with the Father and Son. I adore Thee as the Life of all that live. . . . Through Thee, spring comes after winter and renews all things. That wonderful and beautiful, that irresistible burst into life again, in spite of all obstacles, that awful triumph of nature, is but Thy glorious Presence. Through Thee, Almighty Lord, the angels and saints sing Thee praises in heaven. Through Thee our own dead souls are quickened to serve Thee. From Thee is every good thought and desire, every good purpose, every good effort, every good success. It is by Thee that sinners are turned into saints. It is by Thee the Church is refreshed and strengthened, and champions start forth, and martyrs are carried on to their crown. Through Thee new religious orders, new devotions in the Church come into being; new countries are added to the faith, new manifestations and illustrations are given of the ancient Apostolic creed. I praise and adore Thee, my Sovereign Lord God, the Holy Ghost.

THE FOUNT OF LOVE

Thou art that living love, wherewith the Father and the Son love each other. And Thou art the Author of supernatural love in our hearts—As a fire Thou didst come down from heaven on the day of Pentecost; and as a fire Thou burnest away the dross of sin and vanity in the heart and dost light up the pure flame of devotion and affection. It is Thou who unitest heaven and earth by showing to us the glory and beauty of the Divine Nature, and making us love what is in Itself so winning and transporting. . . .

Man is by nature blind and hardhearted in all spiritual matters; how is he to reach heaven? It is by the flame of Thy grace. It is Thou, O Almighty Paraclete, who hast been and art the strength, the vigor and endurance, of the martyr in the midst of his torments. Thou art the stay of the confessor in his long, tedious, and humiliating toils. Thou art the Fire, by which the preacher wins souls, without thought of himself, in his missionary labors. By Thee we wake up from the death of sin, to exchange the idolatry of the creature for the pure love of the Creator. By Thee we make acts of faith, hope, charity, and contrition. By Thee we live in the atmosphere of earth, proof against its infection. By the fire which Thou didst kindle within us, we pray, and meditate, and do penance. As well could our bodies live, if the sun were extinguished, as our souls, if Thou art away. . . .

My God, teach me so to live, as one who does believe the great dignity, the great sanctity of a temple of the Holy Ghost! Should I not venerate that which Thou dost miraculously feed, and which Thy Coequal Spirit inhabits? My God, who wast nailed to the cross, "pierce Thou my flesh with Thy fear;" crucify my soul and body in all that is sinful in them, and make me pure as Thou art pure.

In Awe

I adore Thee, O almighty Lord, the Paraclete, because Thou in Thy infinite compassion has brought me into this Church, the work of Thy supernatural power. I had no claim on Thee for so wonderful a favor over anyone else in the whole world. There were many men far better than I by nature, gifted with more pleasing natural gifts, and less stained with sin. Yet Thou in Thy inscrutable love for me, hast chosen me and brought me into Thy fold. . . . And thus I owe all to Thy grace.

— V. —

EUCHARIST

To me nothing is so consoling, so piercing,
so thrilling, so overcoming, as the Mass.

Before Thee

He dwells on our altars Himself, the Most Holy, the Most High, in light inaccessible, and Angels fall down before Him there; and out of visible substances and forms He chooses what is choicest to represent and to hold Him. The finest wheat-flour, and the purest wine, are taken as His outward symbols; the most sacred and majestic words minister to the sacrificial rite; altar and sanctuary are adorned decently or splendidly, as our means allow; and the Priests perform their office in befitting vestments, lifting up chaste hearts and holy hands.

Omnipotence in Bonds

When we confess God as omnipotent only, we have gained but a half-knowledge of Him; His is an Omnipotence which can at the same time swathe Itself in infirmity and can become the captive of Its own creatures. He has, if I may so speak, the incomprehensible power of even making Himself weak. We must know Him by His names, Emmanuel and Jesus, to know Him perfectly. . . . He tore open the solid rock; He rose from the tomb; He ascended on High; He is far off from the earth; He is safe from profanation; and the soul and body, which He assumed, partake of course, as far as created nature allows, of the Sovereign Freedom and the Independence of Omnipotence. . . . Does He set such a value on subjection to His creatures, that, before He goes away, on the very eve of His betrayal, He must actually make provision, after death, for perpetuating His captivity to the end of the world?

My Brethren, the great truth is daily before our eyes; He has ordained the standing miracle of His Body and Blood under visible symbols, that He may secure thereby the standing mystery of Omnipotence in bonds.

To My Father

I know He is All-holy, yet I come before Him. I place myself under His pure and piercing eyes, which look me through and through, and discern every trace and every motion of evil within me. Why do I do so? First of all, for this reason. To whom should I go? What can I do better? Who is there in the whole world that can help me? Who that will care for me, or pity me, or have any kind thought of me, if I cannot obtain it of Him? I know He is of purer eyes than to behold iniquity; but I know again that He is All-merciful, and that He so sincerely desirest my salvation that He has died for me. Therefore, though I am in a great strait, I will rather fall into His hands than into those of any creature. . . . I have an instinct within me which leads me to rise and go to my Father, to name the Name of His well-beloved Son, and having named it, to place myself unreservedly in His hands, saying, "If Thou, Lord, wilt be extreme to mark what is done amiss, O Lord, who may abide it! But there is forgiveness with Thee."

A Short Visit

He took bread, and blessed, and made it His Body; He took wine and gave thanks, and made it His Blood; and He gave His priests the power to do what He had done. Henceforth, He is in the hands of sinners once more. Frail, ignorant, sinful man, by the sacerdotal power given to him, compels the presence of the Highest; he lays Him up in a small tabernacle; he dispenses Him to a sinful people. Those who are only just now cleansed from mortal sin, open their lips for Him; those who are soon to return to mortal sin, receive Him into their breasts; those who are polluted with vanity and selfishness and ambition and pride, presume to make Him their guest; the frivolous, the tepid, the worldly-minded, fear not to welcome Him. Alas! alas! even those who wish to be more in earnest, entertain Him with cold and wandering thoughts, and quench that Love which would inflame them with Its own fire, did they but open to It. Such are the best of us; and then for the worst? What shall we say of sacrilege? of His reception into hearts polluted with mortal, unforsaken sin? of those further nameless profanations, which from time to time occur, when unbelief dares to present itself at the Holy Altar, and blasphemously gains possession of Him? . . .

I place myself in the presence of Him, in whose Incarnate Presence I am before I place myself there.

I adore Thee, O my Saviour, present here as God and man, in soul and body, in true flesh and blood.

I acknowledge and confess that I kneel before that Sacred Humanity, which was conceived in Mary's womb, and lay in Mary's bosom; which grew up to man's estate, and by the Sea of Galilee called the Twelve, wrought miracles, and spoke words of wisdom and peace; which in due season hung on the cross, lay in the tomb, rose from the dead, and now reigns in heaven.

I praise and bless, and give myself wholly to Him, who is the true Bread of my soul, and my everlasting joy.

One Eucharistic Hymn

To me nothing is so consoling, so piercing, so thrilling, so overcoming, as the Mass, said as it is among us. I could attend Masses forever, and not be tired. It is not a mere form of words—it is a great action, the greatest action that can be on earth. It is, not the invocation merely, but, if I dare use the word, the evocation of the Eternal. He becomes present on the altar in flesh and blood, before whom angels bow and devils tremble. This is that awful event which is the scope, and the interpretation, of every part of the solemnity. Words are necessary, but as means, not as ends; they are not mere addresses to the throne of grace, they are instruments of what is far higher, of consecration, of sacrifice. They hurry on, as if impatient to fulfil their mission. Quickly they go, the whole is quick, for they are all parts of the integral action, for they are awful words of sacrifice, they are a work too great to delay upon, as when it was said in the beginning, "What thou doest, do quickly." Quickly they pass, for the Lord Jesus goes with them, as He passed along the lake in the days of His flesh, quickly calling first one and then another; quickly they pass, because as the lightning which shineth from one part of the heaven into the other, so is the coming of the Son of Man. Quickly they pass, for they are as the words of Moses, when the Lord came down in the cloud, calling on the name of the Lord as he passed by, "The Lord, the Lord God, merciful and gracious, long suffering and abundant in goodness and truth." And as Moses on the mountain, so we too "make haste to bow our heads to the earth, and adore." So we, all around, each in his place, look out for the great Advent, "waiting for the moving of the water," each in his place, with his own heart, with his own wants, with his own thoughts, with his own intentions, with his own prayers, separate but concordant, watching what is going on, watching its progress, uniting in its consummation; not painfully and hopelessly, following a hard form of prayer from beginning to end, but, like a concert of musical instruments, each different, but concurring in a sweet harmony, we take our part with God's priest, supporting him, yet guided by him. There are little children there, and old men, and simple laborers, and students in seminaries, priests preparing for Mass, priests making their thanksgiving, there are innocent maidens, and there are penitent sinners;

but out of these many minds rises one Eucharistic hymn, and the great action is the measure and the scope of it.

O my God, holiness becometh Thy House, and yet Thou dost make Thy abode in my breast. Thou, Who didst first inhabit Mary's breast, dost come to me. When I say, "Lord, I am not worthy"—Thou whom I am addressing, alone understandest in their fullness the words which I use.

JESUS OUR DAILY SACRIFICE

Our Lord not only offered Himself as a Sacrifice on the cross, but He makes Himself a perpetual, a daily Sacrifice, to the end of time. In the Holy Mass that One Sacrifice on the cross once offered is renewed, continued, applied to our benefit. He seems to say, "My cross was raised up 1800 years ago, and only for a few hours—and very few of My servants were present there—but I intend to bring millions into My Church. For their sakes, then, I will perpetuate My Sacrifice, that each of them may be as though they had severally been present on Calvary. I will offer Myself up day by day to the Father, that every one of My followers may have the opportunity to offer his petitions to Him, sanctified and recommended by the all-meritorious virtue of My passion. Thus I will be a Priest forever, after the order of Melchisedech— My priests shall stand at the altar—but not they, but I rather, will offer. I will not let them offer mere bread and wine, but I Myself will be present upon the altar instead, and I will offer up Myself invisibly, while they perform the outward rite."

MARY RECEIVES HIM

I see thee after the ascension. This is a time of bereavement, but still of consolation. It was still a twilight time, but not a time of grief. The Lord was absent, but He was not on earth, He was not in suffering. Death had no power over Him. And He came to her day by day in the Blessed Sacrifice. I see the Blessed Mary at Mass, and Saint John celebrating. She is waiting for the moment of her Son's Presence: now she converses with Him in the sacred rite; and what shall I say now? She receives Him, to whom once she gave birth. . . .

O Holy Mother, stand by me now at Mass time, when Christ comes to me, as thou didst minister to thy infant Lord—as thou didst hang upon His words when He grew up, as thou wast found under His cross. Stand by me, Holy Mother, that I may gain somewhat of thy purity, thy innocence, thy faith, and He may be the one object of my love and my adoration, as He was of thine.

INVINCIBLE KING

We come before Him in the bright and glad spirit of soldiers who know they are under the leading of an Invincible King, and wait with beating hearts to see what He is about to do; and therefore it is that we adorn our sanctuary, bringing out our hangings and multiplying our lights, as on a day of festival. We know well we are on the winning side, and that the prayers of the poor, the weak, and the despised, merit more, when offered in a true spirit, than all the wisdom and all the resources of the world. The prayers of Saint Pius, and the Holy Rosary said by thousands of the faithful at his bidding, broke forever the domination of the Turks in the great battle of Lepanto. God will give us what we ask, or He will give us something better. In this spirit let us proceed with the holy Mass which we have begun,—in the presence of innumerable witnesses, of God the Judge of all, of Jesus the Mediator of the New Covenant, of His Mother Mary our Immaculate Protectress, of all the Angels of Holy Church, of all the blessed Saints, of Apostles and Evangelists, Martyrs and Confessors, of Holy preachers, holy recluses, holy virgins, of holy innocents taken away before actual sin, and of all other holy souls who have been purified by suffering, and have already reached their heavenly home. . . .

Pray that we may not come short of that destiny to which God calls us; that we may be visited by His effectual grace, enabling us to break the bonds of lukewarmness and sloth, to command our will, to rule our actions through the day, to grow continually in devotion and fervour of spirit, and, while our natural vigour decays, to feel that keener energy which comes from heaven.

SMALL TABERNACLE

Most tender and gentle Lord Jesus, when will my heart have a portion of Thy perfections? When will my hard and stony heart, my proud heart, my unbelieving, my impure heart, my narrow selfish heart, be melted and conformed to Thine? Teach me so to contemplate Thee that I may become like Thee, and to love Thee sincerely and simply as Thou hast loved me.

Thou biddest me love Thee in turn, for Thou hadst loved me. Thou wooest me to love Thee specially, above all others. Thou dost say, "Lovest Thou me more than these?" Why should I not love Thee much, how can I help loving Thee much, whom Thou hast brought so near to Thyself, whom Thou hast so wonderfully chosen out of the world to be Thy own special servant and son?

It was love that brought Thee from heaven, and subjected Thee to the laws of a created nature. It was love alone which was able to conquer Thee, the highest—and bring Thee low. Thou didst die through Thine infinite love of sinners. And it is love which keeps Thee here still, even now that Thou hast ascended on high, in a small tabernacle, imprisoned and exposed to slight, indignity, and insult. My God, I do not know what infinity means—but one thing I see, that Thou art loving to a depth and height far beyond any measurement of mine.

I will trust Thee. Whatever, wherever I am, I can never be thrown away. If I am in sickness, my sickness may serve Thee; in perplexity, my perplexity may serve Thee; if I am in sorrow, my sorrow may serve Thee. Thou doest nothing in vain; Thou mayest prolong my life, Thou mayest shorten it; Thou knowest what Thou art about. Thou mayest take away my friends, throw me among strangers, make me feel desolate, make my spirits sink, hide the future from me—still Thou knowest what Thou art about.

Mighty God, strengthen me with Thy strength, console me with Thy everlasting peace, soothe me with the beauty of Thy countenance; enlighten me with Thy uncreated brightness; purify me with the fragrance of Thy ineffable holiness; give me to drink of the rivers of grace which flow from the Father and the Son, and the Holy Ghost.

NOT MY OWN

My Lord, I offer Thee myself in turn as a sacrifice of thanksgiving. Thou hast died for me, and I in turn make myself over to Thee. I am not my own. Thou hast bought me; I will by my own act and deed complete the purchase. My wish is to be separated from everything of this world; to cleanse myself simply from sin; to put away from me even what is innocent, if used for its own sake, and not for Thine. I put away reputation and honor, and influence, and power, for my praise and strength shall be in Thee. Enable me to carry out what I profess.

A PRIEST FOREVER

I adore Thee, O my Lord God, with the most profound awe for Thy passion and crucifixion, in sacrifice for our sins. Thou didst suffer incommunicable sufferings in Thy sinless soul. Thou wast exposed in Thy innocent body to ignominious torments, to mingled pain and shame. Thou wast stripped and fiercely scourged, Thy sacred body vibrating under the heavy flail as trees under the blast. Thou wast, when thus mangled, hung upon the cross, naked, a spectacle for all to see Thee quivering and dying. Rather, then, than I should perish according to my deserts, Thou wast nailed to the tree and didst die.

Such a sacrifice was not to be forgotten. It was not to be—it could not be—a mere event in the world's history, which was to be done and over, and was to pass away except in its obscure, unrecognized effects. If that great deed was what we believe it to be, what we know it is, it must remain present, though past; it must be a standing fact for all times. . . .

In Thee, O Lord, all things live, and Thou dost give them their food. "The eyes of all hope in Thee." Thou knowest, O my God, Who madest us, that nothing can satisfy us but Thyself, and therefore Thou hast caused Thy own self to be meat and drink to us. Thou most Glorious, and Beautiful, and Strong, and Sweet, Thou didst know well that nothing else would support our immortal natures, our frail hearts, but Thyself; and so Thou didst take a human flesh and blood, that they, as being the flesh and blood of God, might be our life. . . .

To whom should I go but to Thee? Who can save me but Thou? Who can cleanse me but Thou? Who can make me overcome myself but Thou? Who can raise my body from the grave but Thou? Therefore I come to Thee in all these my necessities, in fear, but in faith. . . .

The more I refuse to open my heart to Thee, so much the fuller and stronger be Thy supernatural visitings, and the more urgent and efficacious Thy Presence in me.

THE FOUNT OF MERCY

The Benediction of the Blessed Sacrament is one of the simplest rites of the Church. The priests enter and kneel down; one of them unlocks the tabernacle, takes out the Blessed Sacrament, inserts it upright in a monstrance of precious metal, and sets it in a conspicuous place above the altar, in the midst of lights for all to see. The people then begin to sing; meanwhile the priest twice offers incense to the King of heaven, before whom he is kneeling. Then he takes the monstrance in his hands, and turning to the people blesses them with the Most Holy, in the form of a cross, while the bell is sounded by one of the attendants to call attention to the ceremony. It is our Lord's solemn benediction of His people, as when He lifted up His hands over the children, or when He blessed His chosen ones when He ascended up from Mount Olivet. As sons might come before a parent before going to bed at night, so, once or twice a week, the great family comes before the Eternal Father, after the bustle or toil of the day, and He smiles upon them, and sheds upon them the light of His countenance. It is a full accomplishment of what the priest invoked upon the Israelites, "The Lord bless thee and keep thee; the Lord turn His countenance to thee and give thee peace." Can there be a more touching rite, even in the judgment of those who do not believe in it? How many a man, not a Catholic, is moved on seeing it, to say, "Oh that I did but believe it!" when he sees the priest take up the Fount of Mercy, and the people bent low in adoration!

It is one of the most beautiful, natural, and soothing actions of the Church.

HIS THRONE OVER THE ALTAR

And what the Church urges on us down to this day, saints and holy men down to this day have exemplified. Is it necessary to refer to the lives of the Holy Virgins, who were and are His very spouses, wedded to Him by a mystical marriage, and in many instances visited here by the earnests of that ineffable celestial benediction which is in heaven their everlasting portion? The martyrs, the confessors of the Church, bishops, evangelists, doctors, preachers, monks, hermits, ascetical teachers—have they not, one and all, as their histories show, lived on the very name of Jesus, as food, as medicine, as fragrance, as light, as life from the dead?—as one of them says, *"in aure dulce canticum, in ore mel mirificum, in corde nectar coelicum."*

Nor is it necessary to be a saint thus to feel: this intimate, immediate dependence on Emmanuel, God with us, has been in all ages the characteristic, almost the definition of a Christian. It is the ordinary feeling of Catholic populations; it is the elementary feeling of everyone who has but a common hope of heaven. I recollect, years ago, hearing an acquaintance, not a Catholic, speak of a work of devotion, written as Catholics usually write, with wonder and perplexity, because, (he said) the author wrote as if he had "a sort of personal attachment to our Lord"; "it was as if he had seen Him, known Him, lived with Him, instead of merely professing and believing the great doctrine of the Atonement." It is this same phenomenon which strikes those who are not Catholics, when they enter our churches. Wherefore those spontaneous postures of devotion? why those unstudied gestures? why those abstracted countenances? why that heedlessness of the presence of others? The spectator sees the effect; he cannot understand the cause of it. Why this simple earnestness of worship? We have no difficulty in answering. It is because the Incarnate Savior is present in the tabernacle; and then, when suddenly the hitherto silent church is, as it were, illuminated with the full piercing burst of voices from the whole congregation, it is because He now has gone up upon His throne over the altar, there to be adored. It is the visible sign of the Son of Man which thrills through the congregation, and makes them overflow with jubilation.

SACRED SYMBOL

My God, my Savior, I adore Thy Sacred Heart, for that heart is the seat and source of all Thy tenderest human affections for us sinners. It is the instrument and organ of Thy love. It did beat for us. It yearned over us. It ached for us, and for our salvation. It was on fire through zeal, that the glory of God might be manifested in and by us. It is the channel through which has come to us all Thy overflowing human affection, all Thy divine charity toward us. All Thy incomprehensible compassion for us, as God and Man, as our Creator and our Redeemer and Judge, has come to us, and comes, in one inseparably mingled stream, through that Sacred Heart. O most Sacred symbol and Sacrament of Love, divine and human, in its fullness, Thou didst save me by Thy divine strength, and Thy human affection, and then at length by that wonder-working blood, wherewith Thou didst overflow.

HAVE PEACE

O most sacred, most loving Heart of Jesus, Thou art concealed in the Holy Eucharist, and Thou beatest for us still. Now as then Thou sayest, "With desire I have desired." I worship Thee, then, with all my best love and awe, with my fervent affection, with my most subdued, most resolved will. Thou for a while takest up Thy abode within me! O make my heart beat with Thy Heart. Purify it of all that is earthly, all that is proud and sensual, all that is hard and cruel, of all perversity, of all disorder, of all deadness. So fill it with Thee, that neither the events of the day nor the circumstances of the time may have power to ruffle it; but that in Thy love and Thy fear it may have peace.

CHRISTMAS JOY

The Son of God Most High, who created the worlds, became flesh. . . . What an emptying of His glory to become man! And not only a helpless infant, though that were humiliation enough, but to inherit all the infirmities and imperfections of our nature which were possible to a sinless soul. What are His thoughts, if I may venture to use such language or admit such reflection concerning the Infinite, when human feelings, human sorrows, human wants, first become His? What a mystery is there from first to last in the Son of God becoming man! Yet in proportion to the mystery is the grace and mercy of it; and as is the grace, so is the greatness of the fruit of it. . . .

Let us seek the grace of a cheerful heart, an even temper, sweetness, gentleness, and brightness of mind, as walking in His light and by His grace. Let us pray Him to give us the spirit of ever-abundant, ever-springing love, which overpowers and sweeps away the vexations of life by its own richness and strength, and which above all things unites us to Him who is the fountain and the centre of all mercy, loving kindness, and joy.

—VI.—

BLESSED VIRGIN

It is the boast of the Catholic religion, that it
has the gift of making the . . . heart chaste;
and why is this, but that it gives us Jesus
Christ for our food, and Mary for our nursing
mother? Fulfill this boast in yourselves;
vindicate the glory of your mother Mary;
go to her for the royal heart of innocence.

MOST PURE VIRGIN

To consider the world in its length and breadth, its various history, the many races of man, their starts, their fortunes, their mutual alienation, their conflicts; and their ways, habits, governments, forms of worship; their enterprises, their aimless courses, their random achievements and acquirements, the impotent conclusion of long-standing facts, the tokens so faint and broken of a superintending design, the blind evolution of what turns out to be great powers or truths, the progress of things, as if from unreasoning elements, not towards final causes, the greatness and littleness of man, his far-reaching aims, his short duration, the curtain hung over his futurity, the disappointments of life, the defeat of good, the success of evil, physical pain, mental anguish, the prevalence and intensity of sin, the pervading idolatries, the corruptions, the dreary hopeless irreligion, that condition of the whole race, so fearfully yet exactly described in the Apostle's words, "having no hope and without God in the world"—all this is a vision to dizzy and appal; and inflicts upon the mind the sense of a profound mystery, which is absolutely beyond human solution. What then shall be said to this heart-piercing, reason-bewildering fact? I can only answer, that either there is no Creator, or this living society of men is in a true sense discarded from His presence. . . . The human race is implicated in some terrible aboriginal calamity. It is out of joint with the purposes of its

Creator. This is a fact, a fact as true as the fact of its existence; and thus the doctrine of what is theologically called original sin becomes to me as certain as that the world exists, and as the existence of God. . . .

But Mary never was in this state; she was by the eternal decree of God exempted from it. From eternity, God, the Father, Son, and Holy Ghost, decreed to create the race of man, and, foreseeing the fall of Adam, decreed to redeem the whole race by the Son's taking flesh and suffering on the Cross. He who was born from Eternity was born by an eternal decree to save us in time, and to redeem the whole race; and Mary's redemption was determined in that special manner which we call the Immaculate Conception. It was decreed, not that she should be cleansed from sin, but that she should, from the first moment of her being, be preserved from sin; so that the Evil One never had any part in her. Therefore she was a child of Adam and Eve as if they had never fallen; she did not share with them their sin; she inherited the gifts and graces (and more than those) which Adam and Eve possessed in Paradise. This is her prerogative, and the foundation of all those salutary truths which are revealed to us concerning her. Let us say then with all holy souls, Virgin most pure, conceived without original sin, Mary, pray for us.

SON AND MOTHER TOGETHER

The Church and Satan agreed together in this, that Son and Mother went together; and the experience of the centuries has confirmed their testimony; for Catholics who have honored the Mother still worship the Son, while those, who now have ceased to confess the Son, began then by scoffing at the Mother. . . .

The world grows old, but the Church is ever young. She can, in any time, at her Lord's will, "inherit the Gentiles, and inhabit the desolate cities." "Arise Jerusalem, for thy light is come, and the glory of the Lord is risen upon thee. Behold, darkness shall cover the earth, and a mist the people; but the Lord shall arise upon thee. Lift up thine eyes round about, and see; all these are gathered together, they come to thee; thy sons shall come from afar, and thy daughters shall rise at thy side." "Arise, make haste, my love, my dove, my beautiful one, and come. For the winter is now past, and the rain is over and gone. The flowers have appeared in our land . . . the fig tree hath put forth her green figs; the vines in flower yield their sweet smell. Arise, my love, my beautiful one, and come." It is the time for thy Visitation. Arise, Mary, and go forth in thy strength into that north country, which once was thine own, and take possession of a land which knows thee not. Arise, Mother of God, and with thy thrilling voice, speak to those who labor with child, and are in pain, till the babe of grace leaps within them! Shine on us, dear Lady, with thy bright countenance, like the sun in his strength, *O stella matutina,* O harbinger of peace, till our year is one perpetual May. From thy sweet eyes, from thy pure smile, from thy majestic brow, let ten thousand influences rain down not to confound or overwhelm, but to persuade, to win over thine enemies. O Mary, my hope, O Mother undefiled, fulfill to us the promise of this Spring.

QUICUNQUE CHRISTUM QUAERITIS

O ye who seek the Lord,
　　Lift up your eyes on high,
For there He doth the Sign accord
　　Of His bright majesty.

We see a dazzling sight
　　That shall outlive all time,
Older than depth or starry height,
　　Limitless and sublime.

'Tis He for Israel's fold
　　And heathen tribes decreed,
The King to Abraham pledged of old
　　And his unfailing seed.

Prophets foretold His birth,
　　And witness'd when He came,
The Father speaks to all the earth
　　To hear, and own His name.

To Jesus, who displays
　　To babes His beaming face,
Be, with the Father, endless praise,
　　And with the Spirit of grace. Amen.

LIFE OF DUTIES

[Mary] is not only the great instance of the contemplative life, but also of the practical; and the practical life is at once a life of penance and of prudence, if it is to be well discharged. Now Mary was as full of external work and hard service as any Sister of Charity at this day. Of course her duties varied according to the seasons of her life, as a young maiden, as a wife, as a mother, and as a widow; but still her life was full of duties day by day and hour by hour. As a stranger in Egypt, she had duties towards the poor heathen among whom she was thrown. As a dweller in Nazareth, she had her duties towards her kinsfolk and neighbors. She had her duties, though unrecorded, during those years in which our Lord was preaching and proclaiming His Kingdom.

After He had left this earth, she had her duties towards the Apostles, and especially towards the Evangelists. She had duties towards the Martyrs, and to the Confessors in prison; to the sick, to the ignorant, and to the poor. Afterwards, she had to seek with Saint John another and a heathen country, where her happy death took place. But before that death, how much must she have suffered in her life amid an idolatrous population! . . . It is then, through the pains and sorrows of her earthly pilgrimage that we are able to invoke her as the *Virgo prudentissima*.

SEAT OF WISDOM

Mary has this title in her Litany, because the Son of God, who is also called in Scripture the Word and

Wisdom of God, once dwelt in her, and then, after His birth of her, was carried in her arms and seated in her lap in His first years. Thus, being, as it were, the human throne of Him who reigns in heaven, she is called the Seat of Wisdom. In the poet's words:—

His throne, thy bosom blest,
O Mother undefiled,
That Throne, if aught beneath the skies,
Beseems the sinless Child.

But the possession of her Son lasted beyond His infancy—He was under rule, as Saint Luke tells us, and lived with her in her house till He went forth to preach—that is, for at least a whole thirty years. . . .

Must not also the knowledge which she gained during those many years from His conversation of present, past, and future, have been so large, and so profound, and so diversified, and so thorough, that, though she was a poor woman without human advantages, she must in her knowledge of creation, of the universe, and of history, have excelled the greatest of philosophers, and in her theological knowledge the greatest of theologians, and in her prophetic discernment the most favored of prophets?

GOD'S OWN MOTHER

We are told by Saint Matthew, that after our Lord's death upon the Cross "the graves were opened, and many bodies of the saints that had slept"—that is, slept the sleep of death—"arose, and coming out of the tombs after His Resurrection, came into the Holy

City, and appeared to many." Saint Matthew says, *many* bodies of the saints"—that is, the holy Prophets, Priests, and Kings of former times—rose again in anticipation of the last day.

Can we suppose that Abraham, or David, or Isaias, or Ezechias, should have been thus favored, and not God's own Mother?

THE POWERFUL VIRGIN

By prayer all this may be done, which naturally is impossible. Noe prayed, and God said that there never again should be a flood to drown the race of man. Moses prayed, and ten grievous plagues fell upon the land of Egypt. Josue prayed, and the sun stood still. Samuel prayed, and thunder and rain came in wheat harvest. Elias prayed, and brought down fire from heaven. Eliseus prayed, and the dead came to life. Ezechias prayed, and the vast army of the Assyrians was smitten and perished.

This is why the Blessed Virgin is called Powerful—nay, sometimes, All-powerful, because she has, more than anyone else, more than all the Angels and Saints, this great, prevailing gift of prayer. No one has access to the Almighty as His Mother has; none has merit such as hers.

Her Son will deny her nothing that she asks; and herein lies her power.

HERALDING THE SUN

[Mary] is at once the *Rosa Mystica* and the *Stella Matutina*. Of these two, both of them well suited to her, the Morning Star becomes her best, and that [is] for three reasons. First, the rose belongs to this earth, but the star is placed in high heaven. Mary now has no part in this nether world. No change, no violence from fire, water, earth, or air, affects the stars above; and they show themselves, ever bright, and marvellous, in all regions of this globe, and to all the tribes of men.

And next, the rose has but a short life; its decay is as sure as it was graceful and fragrant in its noon. But Mary, like the stars, abides forever, as lustrous now as she was on the day of her Assumption; as pure and perfect, when her Son comes in judgment, as she is now.

Lastly, it is Mary's prerogative to be the *Morning* Star, which heralds in the sun. She does not shine for herself, or from herself, but she is the reflection of her and our Redeemer, and she glorifies Him. When she appears in the darkness, we know that He is close at hand. He is Alpha and Omega, the First and the Last, the Beginning and the End. Behold He comes quickly, and His reward is with Him, to render to every one according to His works. "Surely I come quickly. Amen. Come, Lord Jesus."

A HIGH MEMORIAL

Kings of the earth, when they have sons born to them, forthwith scatter some large bounty, or raise some high memorial; they honor the day, or the place, or the heralds of the auspicious event, with some corresponding mark of favor; nor did the coming of Emmanuel innovate on the world's established custom. It was a season of grace and prodigy, and these were to be exhibited in a special manner in the person of His Mother. The course of ages was to be reversed; the tradition of evil was to be broken; a gate of light was to be opened amid the darkness, for the coming of the Just;—a Virgin conceived and bore Him. . . .

She began where others end, whether in knowledge or in love. She was from the first clothed in sanctity, destined for perseverance, luminous and glorious in God's sight, and incessantly employed in meritorious acts, which continued till her last breath. Her was emphatically "the path of the just, which, as the shining light, goeth forward and increaseth even to the perfect day"; and sinlessness in thought, word, and deed, in small things as well as great, in venial matter as well as grievous, is surely but the natural and obvious sequel of such a beginning. If Adam might have kept himself from sin in his first state, much more shall we expect immaculate perfection in Mary. . . .

She has no chance place in the Divine Dispensation; the Word of God did not merely come to her and go from her; He did not merely pass through her, as He visits us in Holy Communion. It was no heavenly body which the Eternal Son assumed, fashioned by the angels, and brought down to this lower world; no: He imbibed, He sucked up her blood and her substance into His Divine Person; He became man of her; and received her lineaments and her features, as the appropriate character in which He was to manifest Himself to mankind. The child is like the parent, and we may well suppose that by His likeness to her was manifested her relationship to Him. Her sanctity comes, not only of her being His mother, but also of His being her son.

MARY, MOST PURE

Above all, let us imitate her purity, who, rather than relinquish her virginity, was willing to lose Him for a Son. O my dear children, young men and young women, what need have you of the intercession of the Virgin-mother, of her help, of her pattern, in this respect! What shall bring you forward in the narrow way, if you live in the world, but the thought and patronage of Mary? What shall seal your senses, what shall tranquillise your heart, when sights and sounds of danger are around you, but Mary? What shall give you patience and endurance, when you are wearied out with the length of the conflict with evil, with the unceasing necessity of precautions, with the irksomeness of observing them, with the tediousness of their reception, with the strain upon your mind, with your forlorn and cheerless condition, but a loving communion with her! She will comfort you in your discouragements, solace you in your fatigues, raise you after your falls, reward you for your successes. She will show you her Son, your God and your all. When your spirit within you is excited, or relaxed, or de-pressed, when it loses its balance, when it is rest-less and wayward, when it is sick of what it has, and hankers after what it has not, when your eye is solicited with evil and your mortal frame trembles under the shadow of the tempter, what will bring you to yourself, to peace and health, but the cool breath of the Immaculate and the fragrance of the Rose of Sharon?

It is the boast of the Catholic Religion that it has the gift of making the young heart chaste; and why is this, but that it gives us Jesus Christ for our food, and Mary for our nursing Mother? Fulfill this boast in yourselves; prove to the world that you are fol-lowing no false teaching, vindicate the glory of your Mother Mary, whom the world blasphemes, in the very face of the world, by the simplicity of your own deportment, and the sanctity of your words and deeds. Go to her for the royal heart of innocence. She is the beautiful gift of God, which outshines the fascinations of a bad world, and which no one ever sought in sincerity and was disappointed. She is the personal type and representative image of that spir-itual life and renovation in grace, "without which no one shall see God." "Her spirit is sweeter than honey, and her heritage than the honeycomb. They that eat her shall yet be hungry, and they that drink her shall still thirst. Whoso harkeneth to her shall not be confounded, and they that work by her shall not sin."

GUIDE US HOME

If "God heareth not sinners, but if a man be a worshipper of Him and do His will, him He heareth"; if "the continual prayer of a just man availeth much"; if faithful Abraham was required to pray for Abimelech, "for he was a prophet"; if patient Job was to "pray for his friends," for he had "spoken right things before God"; if meek Moses by lifting up his hands, turned the battle in favor of Israel, against Amelec; why should we wonder at hearing that Mary, the only spotless child of Adam's seed, has a transcendent influence with the God of grace? And if the Gentiles at Jerusalem sought Philip, because he was an Apostle, when they desired access to Jesus, and Philip spoke to Andrew, as still more closely in our Lord's confidence, and then both came to Him, is it strange that the Mother should have power with the Son, distinct in kind from that of the purest angel and the most triumphant saint? If we have faith to admit the Incarnation itself, we must admit it in its fullness; why then should we start at the gracious appointments which arise out of it, or are necessary to it, or are included in it? If the Creator comes on earth in the form of a servant and a creature, why may not His Mother on the other hand rise to be the Queen of heaven, and be clothed with the sun, and have the moon under her feet? . . .

Such art thou Holy Mother, in the creed and in the worship of the Church, the defense of many truths, the grace and smiling light of every devotion. In thee, O Mary, is fulfilled, as we can bear it, an original purpose of the Most High. He once had meant to come on earth in heavenly glory, but we sinned; and then He could not safely visit us, except with a shrouded radiance and a bedimmed Majesty, for He was God. So He came Himself in weakness, not in power; and He sent thee a creature, in His stead, with a creature's comeliness and luster suited to our state. And now thy very face and form, dear Mother, speak to us of the Eternal, not like earthly beauty, dangerous to look upon, but like the morning star, which is thy emblem, bright and musical, breathing purity, telling of heaven, and infusing peace. O harbinger of day! O hope of the pilgrim! lead us still as thou hast led; in the dark night, across the bleak wilderness, guide us on to our Lord Jesus, guide us home.

FAITHFUL

He has given your word that, if we will take Him for our portion and put ourselves into His hands, He will guide us through all trials and temptations, and bring us safe to heaven. And to encourage and inspirit us, He reminds us, in various passages of Scripture, that He is the faithful God, the faithful Creator.

And so, His true saints and servants have the special title of "Faithful," as being true to Him as He is to them; as being simply obedient to His will, zealous for His honor, observant of the sacred interests which He has committed to their keeping. Thus

Abraham is called the Faithful; Moses is declared to be faithful in all his house; David, on this account, is called the "man after God's own heart"; Saint Paul returns thanks that "God accounted him faithful"; and, at the last day, God will say to all those who have well employed their talents, "Well done, good and faithful servant."

Mary, in like manner, is preeminently faithful to her Lord and Son. . . . He is the Fount of grace, and all her gifts are from His goodness. O Mary, teach us ever to worship thy Son as the One Creator, and to be devout to thee as the most highly favored of creatures.

PRAYED FOR HIS MURDERERS

When our Lord came upon earth, He might have created a fresh body for Himself out of nothing— or He might have formed a body for Himself out of the earth as He formed Adam. But He preferred to be born, as other men are born, of a human mother. Why did He do so? He did so to put honor on all those earthly relations and connections which are ours by nature; and to teach us that, though He has begun a new creation, He does not wish us to cast off the old creation, as far as it is not sinful. Hence it is our duty to love and honor our parents, to be affectionate to our brothers, sisters, friends, husbands, wives, not only not less, but even more, than it was man's duty before our Lord came on earth. As we become better Christians, more consistent and zealous servants of Jesus, we shall become only more and more anxious for the good of all around us—our kindred, our friends, our acquaintances, our neighbors, our superiors, our inferiors, our masters, our employers. And this we shall do from the recollection [of] how our Lord loved His Mother. He loves her still in heaven with a special love. He refuses her nothing. We, then, on earth must feel a tender solicitude for all our relations, all our friends, all whom we know or have dealings with. And moreover, we must love not only those who love us, but those who hate us or injure us, that we may imitate Him, who not only was loving to His Mother, but even suffered Judas, the traitor, to kiss Him, and prayed for His murderers on the Cross.

Their Risen Queen

She died in private. It became Him who died for the world, to die in the world's sight; it became the Great Sacrifice to be lifted up on high, as a light that could not be hid. But she, the lily of Eden, who had always dwelt out of the sight of man, fittingly did she die in the garden's shade, and amid the sweet flowers in which she had lived. Her departure made no noise in the world. The Church went about her common duties, preaching, converting, suffering; there were persecutions, there was fleeing from place to place, there were martyrs, there were triumphs; at length the rumor spread abroad that the Mother of God was no longer upon earth. Pilgrims went to and fro; they sought for her relics, but they found them not; did she die at Ephesus? or did she die at Jerusalem? Reports varied; but her tomb could not be pointed out, or if it was found, it was open, and instead of her pure and fragrant body, there was a growth of lilies from the earth which she had touched. So enquirers went home marvelling and waiting for further light. And then it was said how that when her dissolution was at hand, and her soul was to pass in triumph before the judgment-seat of her Son, the Apostles were suddenly gathered together in one place, even in the Holy City, to bear part in the joyful ceremonial; how that they buried her with fitting rites; how that the third day, when they came to the tomb, they found it empty, and angelic choirs with their glad voices were heard singing day and night the glories of their risen Queen. But, however we feel towards the details of this history (nor is there anything in it which will be unwelcome or difficult to piety), so much cannot be doubted, from the consent of the whole Catholic world and the revelations made to holy souls, that, as is befitting, she is, soul and body, with her Son and God in heaven, and that we are enabled to celebrate, not only her death, but her Assumption.

—VII.—

PURGATORY

Let the absolving words be said over
me, and the holy oil sign and seal me.

THE GOLDEN PRISON

Weep not for me, when I am gone,
    Nor spend thy faithful breath
In grieving o'er the spot or hour
    Of all-enshrouding death;

Nor waste in idle praise thy love
    On deeds of head or hand,
Which live within the living Book
    Or else are writ in sand;

But let it be thy best of prayers,
    That I may find the grace
To reach the holy house of toll,
    The frontier penance-place,—

To reach that golden palace bright,
    Where souls elect abide,
Waiting their certain call to heaven,
    With angels at their side;

Where hate, nor pride, nor fear torments
    The transitory guest,
But in the willing agony
    He plunges, and is blest.

And as the fainting patriarch gain'd
    His needful halt mid-way,
And then refresh'd pursued his path,
    Where up the mount it lay,

So pray, that, rescued from the storm
    Of heaven's eternal ire,
I may lie down, then rise again,
    Safe, and yet saved by fire.

PEACE AT LAST

I have lost friends, I have lost the world, but I have gained Him, who gives in Himself houses and brethren and sisters and mothers and children and lands a hundred-fold; I have lost the perishable, and gained the Infinite; I have lost time and gained eternity. . . .

May the day come for all of us, of which Easter is the promise, when that first spring may return to us, and a sweetness which cannot die gladden our garden. . . .

May He, as of old, choose "the foolish things of the world to confound the wise, and the weak things of the world to confound the things which are mighty!" May He support us all the day long, till the shades lengthen, and the evening comes, and the busy world is hushed, and the fever of life is over, and our work is done! Then in His mercy may He give us a safe lodging, and a holy rest, and peace at last!

THE ONLY HAPPINESS

To possess Thee, O Lover of Souls, is happiness, and the only happiness of the immortal soul! To enjoy the sight of Thee is the only happiness of eternity. At present I might amuse and sustain myself with the vanities of sense and time, but they will not last forever. We shall be stripped of them when we pass out of this world. All shadows will one day be gone. And what shall I do then? There will be nothing left to me but the Almighty God. God and my soul will be the only two beings left in the whole world, as far as I am concerned. He will be all in all, whether I wish it or no. What a strait I shall then be in if I do not love Him!

HERE

Thou alone, my dear Lord, art the food for eternity, and Thou alone. Thou only canst satisfy the soul of man. Eternity would be misery without Thee, even though Thou didst not inflict punishment. To see Thee, to gaze on Thee, to contemplate Thee, this alone is inexhaustible. Thou indeed art unchangeable, yet in Thee there are always more glorious depths and more varied attributes to search into; we shall ever be beginning as if we had never gazed upon Thee. In Thy Presence are torrents of delight, which whoso tastes will never let go. This is my true portion, O my Lord, here and hereafter!

FOR ALL ETERNITY

My God, how far am I from acting according to what I know so well! I confess it, my heart goes after shadows. . . . Rouse me from sloth and coldness, and make me desire Thee with my whole heart. Teach me to love meditation, sacred reading, and prayer. Teach

me to love that which shall engage my mind for all
eternity.

Ecce Jam Noctis

Paler have grown the shades of night,
  And nearer draws the day,
Checkering the sky with streaks of light,
  Since we began to pray:

To pray for mercy when we sin,
  For cleansing and release,
For ghostly safety, and within
  For everlasting peace.

Praise to the Father, as is meet,
  Praise to the Only Son,
Praise to the Holy Paraclete,
  While endless ages run.

Happy Death

Times come and go, and man will not believe, that
that is to be which is not yet, or that what now is
only continues for a season, and is not eternity. The
end is the trial; the world passes; it is but a pageant
and a scene; the lofty palace crumbles, the busy city
is mute, the ships of Tarshish have sped away. On
heart and flesh death is coming; the veil is breaking. Departing soul, how hast thou used thy talents,
thy opportunities, the light poured around thee, the
warnings given thee, the grace inspired into thee?

O my Lord and Savior, support me in that hour in the strong arms of Thy sacraments, and by the fresh fragrance of Thy consolations. Let the absolving words be said over me, and the holy oil sign and seal me, and Thy own Body be my food, and Thy Blood my sprinkling; and let my sweet Mother Mary breathe on me, and my angel whisper peace to me, and my glorious saints smile on me; that in them all, and through them all, I may receive the gift of perseverance and die, as I desire to live, in Thy faith, in Thy Church, in Thy service, and in Thy love. Amen.

BID THEM COME TO THEE

Jesu! by that shuddering dread which fell on
     Thee;
Jesu! by that cold dismay which sickened Thee;
Jesu! by that pang of heart which thrilled in Thee;
Jesu! by that mount of sins which crippled Thee;
Jesu! by that sense of guilt which stifled Thee;
Jesu! by that innocence which girdled Thee;
Jesu! by that sanctity which reigned in Thee;
Jesu! by that Godhead which was one with Thee;
Jesu! spare these souls which are so dear to Thee,
Who in prison, calm and patient, wait for Thee;
Hasten, Lord, their hour, and bid them come to
     Thee,
To that glorious Home, where they shall ever gaze
     on Thee.

FOR THE DEAD
(A Hymn)

Help, Lord, the souls which Thou hast made,
    The souls to Thee so dear,
In prison for the debt unpaid
    Of sins committed here.

Those holy souls, they suffer on,
    Resign'd in heart and will,
Until Thy high behest is done,
    And justice has its fill.
For daily falls, for pardon'd crime,
    They joy to undergo
The shadow of Thy cross sublime,
    The remnant of Thy woe.

Help, Lord, the souls which Thou hast made,
    The souls to Thee so dear,
In prison for the debt unpaid
    Of sins committed here.

Oh, by their patience of delay,
    Their hope amid their pain,
Their sacred zeal to burn away
    Disfigurement and stain;
Oh, by their fire of love, not less
    In keenness than the flame,
Oh, by their very helplessness,
    Oh, by Thy own great Name,
Good Jesu, help! sweet Jesu, aid
    The souls to Thee most dear,

In prison for the debt unpaid
    Of sins committed here.

If They Are There

It will be a blessed thing, in your last hour, when flesh and heart are failing, in the midst of the pain, the weariness, the restlessness, the prostration of strength, and the exhaustion of spirits, which then will be your portion, it will be blessed indeed to have [Mary] at your side, more tender than any earthly mother, to nurse you and to whisper peace. It will be most blessed, when the evil one is making his last effort, when he is coming on you in his might to pluck you away from your Father's hand, if he can—it will be blessed indeed if Jesus, if Mary and Joseph are then with you, waiting to shield you from his assaults, and to receive your soul. If they are there, all are there; Angels are there, Saints are there, heaven is there, heaven is begun in you, and the devil has no part in you. That dread day may be sooner or later, you may be taken away young, you may live to fourscore, you may die in your bed, you may die in the open field, but if Mary intercedes for you, that day will find you watching and ready. All things will be fixed to secure your salvation; all dangers will be foreseen, all obstacles removed, all aids provided. The hour will come, and in a moment you shall be translated beyond fear and risk, I shall be translated into a new state where sin is not, nor ignorance of the future, but perfect faith and serene joy, and assurance and love everlasting. . . .

Let us follow the Saints, as they follow Christ; so that, when He comes in judgment, and the wretched world sinks to perdition, "on us sinners, His servants, hoping in the multitude of His mercies He may vouchsafe to bestow some portion and fellowship with His Holy Apostles and Martyrs, with John, Stephen, Matthias, Barnabas, Ignatius, Alexander, Marcelline, Peter, Felicity, Perpetua, Agatha, Lucy, Agnes, Cicely, Anastasia, and all His Saints, not for the value of our merit, but according to the bounty of His pardon, through the same Christ our Lord."

THAT SOONER I MAY RISE

Take me away, and in the lowest deep
    There let me be,
And there in hope the lone night-watches keep,
    Told out for me.
There, motionless and happy in my pain,
    Lone, not forlorn,—
There will I sing my sad perpetual strain,
    Until the morn.
There will I sing, and soothe my stricken breast,
    Which ne'er can cease
To throb, and pine, and languish, till possest
    Of its Sole Peace.
There will I sing my absent Lord and Love:—
    Take me away,
That sooner I may rise, and go above,
And see Him in the truth of everlasting day.

FOR THE FAITHFUL DEPARTED

O God of the spirits of all flesh, O Jesu, Lover of souls, we recommend unto Thee the souls of all those Thy servants, who have departed with the sign of faith and sleep the sleep of peace. We beseech Thee, O Lord and Savior, that, as in Thy mercy to them Thou becamest man, so now Thou wouldst hasten the time, and admit them to Thy presence above. Remember, O Lord, that they are Thy creatures, not made by strange gods, but by Thee, the only Living and True God; for there is no other God but Thou, and none that can equal Thy works. Let their souls rejoice in Thy light, and impute not to them their former iniquities, which they committed through the violence of passion, or the corrupt habits of their fallen nature. For, although they have sinned, yet they always firmly believed in the Father, Son, and Holy Ghost; and before they died, they reconciled themselves to Thee by true contrition and the Sacraments of Thy Church.

O Gracious Lord, we beseech Thee, remember not against them the sins of their youth and their ignorances; but according to Thy great mercy, be mindful of them in Thy heavenly glory. May the heavens be opened to them and the angels rejoice with them. May the Archangel Saint Michael conduct them to Thee. May Thy holy angels come forth to meet them, and carry them to the city of the heavenly Jerusalem. May Saint Peter, to whom Thou gavest the keys of the kingdom of heaven, receive them. May Saint

Paul, the vessel of election, stand by them. May Saint John, the beloved disciple, who had the revelation of the secrets of heaven, intercede for them. May all the holy Apostles, who received from Thee the power of binding and loosing, pray for them. May all the saints and elect of God, who in this world suffered torments for Thy Name, befriend them; that, being freed from the prison beneath, they may be admitted into the glories of that kingdom, where with the Father and the Holy Ghost Thou livest and reignest one God, world without end.

Come to their assistance, all ye saints of God; gain for them deliverance from their place of punishment; meet them, all ye angels; receive these holy souls, and present them before the Lord. Eternal rest give to them, O Lord. And may perpetual light shine on them.

May they rest in peace. Amen.

To Reap in Joy

Can we religiously suppose that the blood of our martyrs, three centuries ago and since, shall never receive its recompense? Those priests, secular and regular, did they suffer for no end? or rather for an end which is not yet accomplished? The long imprisonment, the fetid dungeon, the weary suspense, the tyrannous trial, the barbarous sentence, the savage execution, the rack, the gibbet, the knife, the caldron, the numberless tortures of those holy victims, O my God, are they to have no reward? Are Thy martyrs to cry from under Thine altar for their loving vengeance on this guilty people, and to cry in vain? Shall they lose life, and not gain a better life for the children of those who persecuted them? Is this Thy way, O my God, righteous and true? Is it according to Thy promise, O King of saints, if I may dare talk to Thee of justice? Didst not Thou Thyself pray for Thine enemies upon the cross, and convert them? Did not Thy first martyr win Thy great Apostle, then a persecutor, by his loving prayer? And in that day of trial and desolation for England, when hearts were pierced through and through with Mary's woe, at the crucifixion of Thy Body mystical, was not every tear that flowed, and every drop of blood that was shed, the seeds of a future harvest, when they who sowed in sorrow were to reap in joy?

Jam Sol Recedit Igneus

The red sun is gone,
    Thou Light of the heart,
Blessed Three, Holy One,
To Thy servants a sun
    Everlasting impart.
There were Lauds in the morn,
    Here are Vespers at even;
Oh, may we adorn
Thy temple new born
    With our voices in Heaven.
To the Father be praise,
    And praise to the Son

And the Spirit always,
While the infinite days
   Of eternity run.

THY PRESENCE

What a day will that be when I am thoroughly cleansed from all impurity and sin, and am fit to draw near to my Incarnate God in His palace of light above! What a morning, when having done with all penal suffering, I see Thee for the first time with these very eyes of mine, I see Thy countenance, gaze upon Thy eyes and gracious lips without quailing, and then kneel down with joy to kiss Thy feet, and am welcomed into Thy arms. O my only true lover, the only lover of my soul, Thee will I love now, that I may love Thee then. . . . O my Lord, what a day when I shall have done once for all with all sins, venial as well as mortal, and shall stand perfect and acceptable in Thy sight, able to bear Thy presence, nothing shrinking from Thy eye, not shrinking from the pure scrutiny of angels and archangels, when I stand in their midst and they around me.

LOVEST THOU ME?

Thou askest us to love Thee, O my God, and Thou art Thyself Love. There was one attribute of Thine which Thou didst exercise from eternity, and that was Love. We hear of no exercise of Thy power whilst Thou wast alone, nor of Thy justice before there were creatures on their trial; nor of Thy wisdom before the acts and works of Thy Providence; but from eternity Thou didst love, for Thou art not only One but Three. The Father loved from eternity His only begotten Son, and the Son returned to Him an equal love. And the Holy Ghost is that Love in substance, wherewith the Father and the Son love one another. This, O Lord, is Thine ineffable and special blessedness. It is love. I adore Thee, O my infinite Love!

RESIGNATION

My God, Thou seest me; I cannot see myself. Were I ever so good a judge about myself, ever so unbiassed, and with ever so correct a rule of judging, still, from my very nature, I cannot look at myself and view myself truly and wholly. But Thou, as Thou comest to me, contemplatest me. . . . Ah, Lord, we know not what is good for us, and what is bad. We cannot foretell the future, nor do we know, when Thou comest to visit us, in what form Thou wilt come. And therefore, we leave it all to Thee. Do Thou Thy good pleasure to us and in us. Let us ever look at Thee, and do Thou look upon us, and give us the grace of Thy bitter Cross and Passion, and console us in Thy own way and at Thy own time. . . .

I believe, O my Savior, that Thou knowest just what is best for me. I believe that Thou lovest me better than I love myself, that Thou art all-wise in Thy Providence, and all-powerful in Thy protection. I am as ignorant as Peter was as to what is to happen to me in time to come; but I resign myself entirely to my ignorance, and thank Thee with all my heart that Thou hast taken me out of my own keeping, and, instead of putting such a serious charge upon me, hast bidden me put myself into Thy hands. I can ask nothing better than this, to be Thy care, not my own. . . .

O my God, Thou and Thou alone art all-wise and all-knowing! Every event of my life is the best for me that could be, for it comes from Thee. Thou dost bring me on year by year, by Thy wonderful Providence, from youth to age, with the most perfect wisdom, and with the most perfect love. . . .

I will wait on Thee for Thy guidance, and on obtaining it, I will act upon it in simplicity and without fear. And I promise that I will not be impatient, if at any time I am kept by Thee in darkness and perplexity; nor will I ever complain or fret if I come into any misfortune or anxiety.

IN THY HANDS

I cry out to Thee, and intreat Thee, first that Thou wouldst keep me from myself, and from following any will but Thine. Next I beg of Thee, that in Thy infinite compassion Thou wouldst temper Thy will to me, that it may not be severe, but indulgent to me. Visit me not, O my loving Lord—if it be not wrong so to pray—visit me not with those trying visitations which saints alone can bear! Still I leave all in Thy hands, my dear Savior—I bargain for nothing. Only, if Thou shalt bring heavier trial on me, give me more grace—flood me with the fulness of Thy strength and consolation, that they may work in me not death, but life and salvation.

— VIII. —

CONFESSION

If there is a heavenly idea in the Catholic Church, looking at it simply as an idea, surely, next after the Blessed Sacrament, Confession is such.

CONFESSION
(Preparation for)

How many are the souls in distress, anxiety, or loneliness, whose one need is to find a being to whom they can pour out their feelings unheard by the world? Tell them out they must; they cannot tell them out to those whom they see every hour. They want to tell them and not to tell them; and they want to tell them out, yet be as if they be not told; they wish to tell them to one who is strong enough to bear them, yet not too strong to despise them; they wish to tell them to one who can at once advise and can sympathize with them, they wish to relieve themselves of a load, to gain a solace, to receive the assurance that there is one who thinks of them, and one to whom in thought they can recur, to whom they can betake themselves, if necessary from time to time, while they are in the world. How many a Protestant's heart would leap at the news of such a benefit, putting aside all distinct ideas of a sacramental ordinance, or of a grant of pardon and the conveyance of a grace! If there is a heavenly idea in the Catholic Church, looking at it simply as an idea, surely, next after the Blessed Sacrament, Confession is such. And such is it ever found in fact—the very act of kneeling, the low and contrite voice, the sign of the cross hanging, so to say, over the head bowed low, and the words of peace and blessing. Oh, what a soothing charm is there, which the world can neither give nor take away! Oh, what piercing, heart-subduing tranquility, provoking tears of joy, is poured almost substantially and physically upon the soul, the oil of gladness, as Scripture calls it, when the penitent at length rises, his God reconciled to him, his sins rolled away forever! This is Confession as it is in fact.

SUMMAE PARENS CLEMENTIAE

Father of mercies infinite,
  Ruling all things that be,
Who, shrouded in the depth and height,
  Art One, and yet art Three;

Accept our chants, accept our tears,
  A mingled stream we pour;
Such stream the laden bosom cheers,
  To taste Thy sweetness more.

Purge Thou with fire the o'ercharged mind,
  Its sores and wounds profound;
And with the watcher's girdle bind
  The limbs which sloth has bound.

That they who with their chants by night
  Before Thy presence come,
All may be fill'd with strength and light
  From their eternal home.

Grant this, O Father, Only Son,
  And Holy Spirit, God of Grace;
To Whom all glory, Three in One,
  Be given in every time and place.

His Son's Merits

Gloom is no Christian temper; that repentance is not real which has not love in it; that self-chastisement is not acceptable which is not sweetened by faith and cheerfulness. We must live in sunshine, even when we sorrow; we must live in God's presence, we must not shut ourselves up in our own hearts, even when we are reckoning up our past sins. . . . [We must] look abroad into this fair world, which God made "very good," while we mourn over the evil which Adam brought into it. We must hold communion with what we see there while we seek Him who is invisible; we must admire it while we abstain from it; acknowledge God's love while we deprecate His wrath; confess that, many as are our sins, His grace is greater. Our sins are more in number than the hairs of our head; yet even the hairs of our head are all numbered by You. You count our sins, and, as You count, so can You forgive; for that reckoning, great though it be, comes to an end; but Your mercies fail not, and Your Son's merits are infinite.

To Serve Thee

Thou, O my God, hast a claim on me, and I am wholly Thine! Thou art the Almighty Creator, and I am Thy workmanship. I am the work of Thy Hands, and Thou art my owner. As well might the axe or the hammer exalt itself against its framer, as I against Thee. Thou owest me nothing; I have no rights in respect to Thee, I have only duties. I depend on Thee for life, and health, and every blessing every moment. If Thou withdraw Thy breath from me for a moment, I die. I am wholly and entirely Thy property and Thy work, and my one duty is to serve Thee.

OUGHT TO BE

O my God, I confess that before now I have utterly forgotten this, and that I am continually forgetting it! I have acted many a time as if I were my own master, and turned from Thee rebelliously. I have acted according to my own pleasure, not according to Thine. I do not understand how dreadful sin is—and I do not hate it, and fear it, as I ought. I have no horror of it, or loathing. I do not turn from it with indignation, as being an insult to Thee, but I trifle with it, and, even if I do not commit great sins, I have no great reluctance to do small ones. O my God, what a great and awful difference is there between what I am and what I ought to be!

AGAINST THEE HAVE I SINNED

I know, O Lord, that according to the greatness of the person offended against, the greater is the offence. Yet I do not fear to offend Thee, whom to offend is to offend the infinite God. . . . To sin is to insult Thee in the grossest of all conceivable ways. This then, O my soul! is what the sinfulness of sin consists in. It is lifting up my hand against my infinite Benefactor, against my

Almighty Creator, Preserver and Judge—against Him in whom all majesty and glory and beauty and reverence and sanctity center; against the one only God. . . . Time is short, eternity is long. Put not from you what you have here found; regard it not as a matter of present enthusiasm; seduce not yourself with the imagination that it comes of disappointment, or restlessness, or wounded feeling, or undue sensibility, or other weakness; wrap not yourself round in the associations of years past, nor determine that to be truth which you wish to be so, nor make an idol of cherished commiserations. Time is short, eternity is long.

PARDON!

O my God, I am utterly confounded to think of the state in which I lie! What will become of me if Thou art severe? What is my life, O my dear and merciful Lord, but a series of offences, little or great, against Thee! O what great sins I have committed against Thee before now—and how continually in lesser matters I am sinning! O my Lord Jesus, whose love for me has been so great as to bring Thee down from heaven to save me, teach me, dear Lord, my sin— teach me its heinousness—teach me truly to repent of it—and pardon it in Thy great mercy!

REJOICE IN THEE

O mighty God! O God of love! it is too much! it broke the heart of Thy sweet Son Jesus to see the misery of man spread out before His eyes. He died by it as well as for it. And we, too, in our measure, our eyes ache, and our hearts sicken, and our heads reel, when we but feebly contemplate it. O most tender heart of Jesus, why wilt Thou not end, when wilt Thou end, this ever-growing load of sin and woe? When wilt Thou chase away the devil into his own hell, and close the pit's mouth, that Thy chosen may rejoice in Thee, quitting the thought of those who perish in their wilfulness?

Consors Paterni Luminis

O God from God, and Light from Light,
    Who art Thyself the day,
Our chants shall break the clouds of night;
    Be with us while we pray.

Chase Thou the gloom that haunts the mind,
    The thronging shades of hell,
The sloth and drowsiness that bind
    The senses with a spell.

Lord, to their sins indulgent be,
    Who, with this hour forlorn,
By faith in what they do not see,
    With songs prevent the morn.

Grant this, O Father, Only Son,
    And Spirit, God of grace,
To whom all worship shall be done
    In every time and place.

EVIL OF SIN

My God, I know that Thou didst create the whole universe. The innumerable stars which fill the firmament, and the very elements out of which the earth is made, all are carried through their courses and their operations in perfect concord; but much higher was the concord which reigned in heaven when the Angels were first created. Then it was that suddenly was discovered a flaw or a rent in one point of this most delicate and exquisite web—and it extended and unravelled the web, till a third part of it was spoilt; and then again a similar flaw was found in human kind, and it extended over the whole race. This dreadful evil, destroying so large a portion of all God's works, is sin. . . .

My God, such is sin in Thy judgment; what is it in the judgment of the world? A very small evil or none at all. In the judgment of the Creator it is that which has marred His spiritual work; it is a greater evil than though the stars got loose, and ran wild in heaven, and chaos came again. But man, who is the guilty one, calls it by soft names. He explains it away. The world laughs at it, and is indulgent of it; and, as to its deserving eternal punishment, it rises up indignant at the idea, and rather than admit it, would deny the God who has said it does. O my soul, consider carefully the great difference between the view of sin taken by Almighty God and the world! . . .

Dear Lord, Thou didst suffer in no ordinary way, but unheard-of and extreme torments! The all-blessed Lord suffered the worst and most various of pains. This is the corner truth of the Gospel; it is the one foundation, Jesus Christ and He crucified. I know it, O Lord, I believe it, and I put it steadily before me.

HATRED OF SIN

Why is this strange anomaly in the face of nature? Does God do things for naught? No, my soul, it is sin; it is thy sin, which has brought the Everlasting down upon earth to suffer. Hence I learned how great an evil sin is. The death of the Infinite is its sole measure. Here then I understand best how horrible a thing sin is. It is horrible, because through it have come upon men all those evils whatever they are, with which the earth abounds. It is more horrible, in that it has nailed the Son of God to the accursed tree. My dear Lord and Saviour, how can I make light of that which has had such consequences! Henceforth I will, through Thy grace, have deeper views of sin than before. . . . Give me a deep-rooted, intense hatred of sin. . . .

My God, I have had experience enough [of] what a dreadful bondage sin is. . . . It is a heavy weight which cripples me—and what will be the end of it? By Thy all-precious merits, by Thy Almighty power, I intreat Thee, O my Lord, to give me life and sanctity and strength! *Deus sanctus*, give me holiness; *Deus fortis*, give me strength; *Deus immortalis*, give me perseverance.

ONE SINGLE VENIAL SIN

Knowledge is one thing, virtue is another; good sense is not conscience, refinement is not humility, nor is largeness and justness of view faith. Philosophy, however enlightened, however profound, gives no command over the passions, no influential motives, no vivifying principles. . . .

Quarry the granite rock with razors, or moor the vessel with a thread of silk; then may I hope with such keen and delicate instruments as human knowledge and human reason to contend against those giants, the passion and the pride of man. . . .

The Church aims, not at making a show, but at doing a work. She regards this world, and all that is in it, as a mere shadow, as dust and ashes, compared with the value of one single soul. She holds that, unless she can, in her own way, do good to souls, it is no use her doing anything; she holds that it were better for sun and moon to drop from heaven, for the earth to fail, than that one soul, I will not say, should be lost, but should commit one single venial sin, should tell one wilful untruth.

TO SIN NO MORE

I beg Thee, O my dear Savior, to recover me! Thy grace alone can do it. I cannot save myself, I cannot recover my lost ground. I cannot turn to Thee, I cannot please Thee, or save my soul without Thee. I shall go from bad to worse, I shall fall from Thee entirely, I shall quite harden myself against my neglect of duty, if I rely on my own strength. I shall worship some idol of my own framing instead of Thee, the only true God and my Maker, unless Thou hinder it by Thy grace. O my dear Lord, hear me! I have lived long enough in this undecided, wavering, unsatisfactory state. I wish to be Thy good servant. I wish to sin no more. Be gracious to me, and enable me to be what I know I ought to be.

A THANKSGIVING
(After Confession)

Lord, in this dust Thy sovereign voice
    First quicken'd love divine;
I am all Thine,—Thy care and choice,
    My very praise is Thine.

I praise Thee, while Thy providence
    In childhood frail I trace,
For blessings given, ere dawning sense
    Could seek or scan Thy grace;

Blessings in boyhood's marvelling hour,
    Bright dreams, and fancyings strange;
Blessings, when reason's awful power
    Gave thought a bolder range.

Yet, Lord, in memory's fondest place
    I shrine those seasons sad,
When, looking up, I saw Thy face
    In kind austereness clad.

—IX.—

SAINTS

Blessed shall you and I be . . . if we
learn to live now in the presence of
Saints and Angels, who are to be our
everlasting companions hereafter.

Kyrie Eleison, Christe Eleison, Kyrie Eleison

Holy Mary, pray for me.
All holy angels, pray for me.
Choirs of the righteous, pray for me.
Holy Abraham, pray for me.
Saint John Baptist, Saint Joseph, pray for me.
Saint Peter, Saint Paul, Saint Andrew, Saint John,
All Apostles, all Evangelists, pray for me.
All holy Disciples of the Lord, pray for me.
All holy Innocents, pray for me.
All holy Martyrs, all holy Confessors,
All holy Hermits, all holy Virgins,
All ye saints of God, pray for me.

My Guardian Angel Prays for Me

O Lord, how wonderful in depth and height,
　　But most in man, how wonderful Thou art!
With what a love, what soft persuasive might
　　Victorious o'er the stubborn fleshy heart,
Thy tale complete of saints Thou dost provide,
To fill the throne which angels lost through pride.

Man lay a grovelling babe upon the ground,
　　Polluted in the blood of his first sire,
With his whole essence shattered and unsound,
　　And, coiled around his heart, a demon dire,
Which was not of his nature, but had skill
To bind and form his opening mind to ill.

Then was I sent from heaven to set right
    The balance of his soul of truth and sin,
And I have waged a long relentless fight,
    Resolved that death-environed spirit to win,
Which from its fallen state, when all was lost,
Had been repurchased at so dread a cost.
Oh, what a shifting parti-colored scene
    Of hope and fear, of triumph and dismay,
Of recklessness and penitence, has been
    The history of that dreary, lifelong fray!
And oh, the grace to nerve him and to lead,
How patient, prompt, and lavish at his need!

O man, strange composite of heaven and earth!
    Majesty dwarfed to baseness! fragrant flower
Running to poisonous seed! and seeming worth
    Cloaking corruption! weakness mastering
        power!
Who never art so near to crime and shame,
As when thou hast achieved some deed
    of name;

How should ethereal natures comprehend
    A thing made up of spirit and of clay,
Were we not tasked to nurse it and to tend,
    Linked one to one throughout its
        mortal day?
More than the Seraph in his height of place,
The Angel-guardian knows and loves the ransomed
    race.

INCOMMUNICABLE GLORY

The devotions then to Angels and Saints as little interfered with the incommunicable glory of the Eternal, as the love which we bear our friends and relations, our tender human sympathies, are inconsistent with that supreme homage of the heart to the Unseen, which really does but sanctify and exalt, not jealously destroy, what is of earth.

GUARDIAN ANGEL

My oldest friend, mine from the hour
    When first I drew my breath;
My faithful friend, that shall be mine,
    Unfailing, till my death;

Thou hast been ever at my side;
    My Maker to thy trust
Consign'd my soul, what time He framed
    The infant child of dust.

No beating heart in holy prayer,
    No faith, inform'd aright
Gave me to Joseph's tutelage,
    Or Michael's conquering might.

Thou wast my sponsor at the font;
    And thou, each budding year,
Didst whisper elements of truth
    Into my childish ear.

And when, ere boyhood yet was gone,
   My rebel spirit fell,
Ah! thou didst see, and shudder too,
   Yet bear each deed of Hell.

And then in turn, when judgments
      came,
   And scared me back again,
Thy quick soft breath was near to soothe
   And hallow every pain.

Oh! who of all thy toils and cares
   Can tell the tale complete,
To place me under Mary's smile,
   And Peter's royal feet!

And thou wilt hang about my bed,
   When life is ebbing low;
Of doubt, impatience, and of gloom,
   The jealous sleepless foe.

Mine, when I stand before the Judge;
   And mine, if spared to stay
Within the golden furnace, till
   My sin is burn'd away.

And mine, O Brother of my soul,
   When my release shall come;
Thy gentle arms shall lift me then,
   Thy wings shall waft me home.

ANGEL GUARDIAN

The world now vainly thinks it knows more than it did, and that it has found the real causes of the things it sees, still may we say, with grateful and simple hearts, "O mountains and hills, green things upon the earth, bless ye the Lord, praise Him, and magnify Him for ever." Thus, whenever we look abroad, we are reminded of those most gracious and holy beings, the servants of the Holiest, who deign to minister to the heirs of salvation. Every breath of air and ray of light and heat, every beautiful prospect, is, as it were, the skirts of their garments, the waving of the robes of those whose faces see God in Heaven.

PATRON SAINT

Be with us, who are thy children and thy clients; and, with thy greater power with God, and with thy more intimate insight into our needs and our dangers, guide us along the path which leads to God and to thee. Be to us a good father; make our priests blameless and beyond reproach or scandal; make our children obedient, our youth prudent and chaste, our heads of families wise and gentle, our old people cheerful and fervent, and build us up, by thy powerful intercessions, in faith, hope, charity, and all virtues. Amen.

TWO ARCHANGELS

The two Archangels who have a special office in the Gospel are Saint Michael and Saint Gabriel—and both of them are associated in the history of the Incarnation with Mary; Saint Gabriel, when the Holy Ghost came down upon her; and Saint Michael, when the Divine Child was born.

Saint Gabriel hailed her as "full of grace," and as "Blessed among women," and announced to her that the Holy Ghost would come down upon her, and that she would bear a Son who would be the Son of the Highest.

Of Saint Michael's ministry to her, on the birth of that Divine Son, we learn in the Apocalypse, written by the Apostle Saint John. Hardly was He born when He was assaulted by the powers of the world who wished to destroy Him. Herod sought to take His life, but he was defeated by Saint Joseph's carrying His Mother and Him off into Egypt. But Saint John in the Apocalypse tells us that Michael and his angels were the real guardians of Mother and Child, then and on other occasions.

First, Saint John saw in vision "a great sign in heaven" (meaning by "heaven" the Church, or Kingdom of God), "a woman clothed with the sun, and with the moon under her feet, and on her head a crown of twelve stars"; and when she was about to be delivered of her Child there appeared "a great red dragon," that is, the evil spirit, ready "to devour her son" when He should be born. The Son was preserved by His own Divine power, but next the evil spirit persecuted her; Saint Michael, however, and his angels came to the rescue and prevailed against him.

"There was a great battle," says the sacred writer; "Michael and his angels fought with the dragon, and the dragon fought and his angels; and that great dragon was cast out, the old serpent, who is called the devil." Now, as then, the Blessed Mother of God has hosts of angels who do her service; and she is their Queen.

SAINT MICHAEL
(A Hymn)

Thou champion high
Of Heaven's imperial Bride,
For ever waiting on her eye,
Before her onward path, and at her side,
In war her guard secure, by night her ready guide!

To thee was given,
When those false angels rose
Against the Majesty of Heaven,
To hurl them down the steep, and on them close
The prison where they roam in hopeless unrepose.

Thee, Michael, thee,
When sight and breathing fail,
The disembodied soul shall see;
The pardon'd soul with solemn joy shall hail,
When holiest rites are spent, and tears no more avail.

And thou, at last,
When time itself must die,

Shalt sound that dread and piercing blast,
To wake the dead, and rend the vaulted sky,
And summon all to meet the Omniscient Judge on
    high.

A Short Road to Perfection

It is the saying of holy men that, if we wish to be perfect, we have nothing more to do than to perform
the ordinary duties of the day well. A short road to
perfection—short, not because easy, but because
pertinent and intelligible. There are no short ways to
perfection, but there are sure ones.

I think this is an instruction which may be of
great practical use to persons like ourselves. It is easy
to have vague ideas what perfection is, which serve
well enough to talk about, when we do not intend to
aim at it; but as soon as a person really desires and
sets about seeking it himself, he is dissatisfied with
anything but what is tangible and clear, and consti-
tutes some sort of direction toward the practice of it.

We must bear in mind what is meant by perfection. It does not mean any extraordinary service,
anything out of the way, or especially heroic—not all
have the opportunity of heroic acts, of sufferings—
but it means what the word perfection ordinarily
means. By perfect we mean that which has no flaw
in it, that which is complete, that which is consistent, that which is sound—we mean the opposite to
imperfect. As we well know what imperfection in re-

ligious service means, we know by the contrast what is meant by perfection.

He, then, is perfect who does the work of the day perfectly, and we need not go beyond this to seek for perfection. You need not go out of the *round* of the day.

I insist on this because I think it will simplify our views, and fix our exertions on a definite aim. If you ask me what you are to do in order to be perfect, I say, first—Do not lie in bed beyond the due time of rising; give your first thoughts to God; make a good visit to the Blessed Sacrament; say the Angelus devoutly; eat and drink to God's glory; say the Rosary well; be recollected; keep out bad thoughts; make meditation well; examine yourself daily; go to bed in good time, and you are already perfect.

MEET MY GOD

Earth must fade away from our eyes, and we must anticipate the great and solemn truth, which we shall not fully understand until we stand before God in judgment, that to us there are but two beings in the whole world, God and ourselves. The sympathy of others, the pleasant voice, the glad eye, the smiling countenance, the thrilling heart, which at present are our very life, all will be away from us when Christ comes in judgment. Every one will have to think of himself. Every eye shall see Him; every heart will be full of Him. He will speak to every one; and every one will be rendering to Him his own account. By self-restraint, by abstinence, by prayer, by meditation, by recollection, by penance, we now anticipate in our measure that dreadful season. By thinking of it beforehand, we hope to mitigate its terrors when it comes. By humbling ourselves now, we hope to escape humiliation then. By owning our faults now, we hope to avert the disclosures of that day. By judging ourselves now, we hope to be spared that judgment which mercy tempers not. We prepare now to meet our God; we retire, as it were, to our sick room, and put our house in order. . . . We leave the goods of earth before they leave us.

THE IDEA OF A SAINT

Very various are the Saints, their very variety is a token of God's workmanship; but however various, and whatever was their special line of duty, they have been heroes in it; they have attained such noble self-command, they have so crucified the flesh, they have so renounced the world; they are so meek, so gentle, so tenderhearted, so merciful, so sweet, so cheerful, so full of prayer, so diligent, so forgetful of injuries; they have attained such great and continued pains, they have persevered in such vast labors, they have made such valiant confessions, they have wrought such abundant miracles, they have been blessed with such strange successes, that they have set up a standard before us of truth, of magnanimity, of holiness, of love. They are not always our examples, we are not always bound to follow them;

not more than we are bound to obey literally some of our Lord's precepts, such as turning the cheek or giving away the coat; not more than we can follow the course of the sun, moon, or stars in the heaven; but though not always our examples, they are always our standard of right and good; they are raised up to be monuments and lessons, they remind us of God, they introduce us into the unseen world, they teach us what Christ loves, they track out for us the way which leads heavenward. They are to us who see them, what wealth, notoriety, rank, and name are to the multitude of men who live in darkness—objects of our veneration and of our homage.

LAUDABILIS NUMERUS

From the time of His birth we may suppose [Jesus] held communion with the spirits of the Old Fathers, who had prepared His coming and prophesied of it. On one occasion He was seen all through the night, conversing with Moses and Elias, and that conversation was about His Passion. What a field of thought is thus opened to us, of which we know how little. When He passed whole nights in prayer, it was greater refreshment to soul and body than sleep. Who could support and (so to say) reinvigorate the Divine Lord better than that "*laudabilis numerus*" of Prophets of which He was the fulfilment and antitype? Then He might talk with Abraham who saw His day, or Moses who spoke to Him; or with His especial types, David and Jeremias; or with those who spoke most of Him, as Isaias and Daniel. And here was a fund of great sympathy. When He came up to Jerusalem to suffer, He might be met in spirit by all the holy priests, who had offered sacrifices in shadow of Him; just as now the priest recalls in Mass the sacrifices of Abel, Abraham, and Melchisedech, and the fiery gift which purged the lips of Isaias, as well as holding communion with the Apostles and martyrs.

A GUEST

The Holy Baptist was separated from the world. He was a Nazarite. He went out from the world, and placed himself over against it, and spoke to it from his vantage ground, and called it to repentance. Then went out all Jerusalem to him into the desert, and he confronted it face to face. But in his teaching he spoke of One who should come to them and speak to them in a far different way. He should not separate Himself from them, He should not display Himself as some higher being, but as their brother, as of their flesh and of their bones, as one among many brethren, as one of the multitude and amidst them; nay, He was among them already.—"There hath stood One in the midst of you, whom you know not." That greater One called Himself the Son of man—He was content to be taken as ordinary in all respects, though He was the Highest. Saint John and the other Evangelists, though so different in the character of their accounts of Him, agree most strikingly here. The Baptist says, "There is in the midst of you One whom you know not." Next we read of his pointing Jesus out privately, not to crowds, but to one or two of his own religious followers; then of their seeking Jesus and being allowed to follow Him home. At length Jesus begins to disclose Himself and to manifest His glory in miracles; but where? At a marriage feast, where there was often excess, as the architriclinus implies. And how? In adding to the wine, the instrument of such excess, when it occurred. He was at that marriage feast not as a teacher, but as a guest, and (so to speak) in a social way, for He was with His mother.

SAINT JOHN THE BAPTIST

Whom can we conceive of such majestic and severe sanctity as the Holy Baptist? He had a privilege which reached near upon the prerogative of the Most Blessed Mother of God; for, if she was conceived without sin, at least without sin he was born. She was all-pure, all-holy, and sin had no part in her; but Saint John was in the beginning of his experience a partaker of Adam's curse; he lay under God's wrath, deprived of that grace which Adam had received, and which is the life and strength of human nature. Yet as soon as Christ, his Lord and Savior, came to him, and Mary saluted his own mother, Elizabeth, forthwith the grace of God was given him, and the original guilt was wiped away from his soul. And therefore it is that we celebrate the nativity of Saint John: nothing unholy does the Church celebrate; not Saint Peter's, nor Saint Paul's, nor Saint Augustine's, nor Saint Gregory's, nor Saint Bernard's, nor Saint Aloysius's, nor the nativity of any other saint, however glorious, because they were all born in sin. She celebrates their conversions, their prerogatives, their martyrdoms, their deaths, their translations, but not their birth, because in no case was it holy. Three nativities alone does she commemorate: our Lord's, His Mother's, and lastly, Saint John's. What a special gift was this, my brethren, separating the Baptist off, and distinguishing him from all prophets and preachers, whoever lived, however holy, except perhaps the prophet Jeremias! And such as was his commencement, was the course of life. He was carried away by the Spirit into the desert, and there he lived on the simplest fare, in the rudest clothing, in the caves of wild beasts, apart from men, for thirty years, leading a life of mortification and of meditation, till he was called to preach penance, to proclaim the Christ and to baptize Him, and then having done his work, and having left no act of sin on record, he was laid aside as an instrument which had lost its use, and languished in prison until he was suddenly cut off by the sword of the executioner. Sanctity is the one idea of him impressed upon us from the first to the last; a most marvelous saint, a hermit from his childhood, then a preacher to a fallen people, and then a martyr. Surely such a life fulfills the expectation which the salutation of Mary raised concerning him before his birth.

SAINT JOHN THE EVANGELIST

Yet still more beautiful, and almost as majestic, is the image of his namesake, that great Apostle, Evangelist, and Prophet of the Church, who came so early into Our Lord's chosen company, and lived so long after his fellows. We can contemplate him in his youth and in his venerable age; and on his whole life, from first to last, as his special gift, is marked purity. He is the virgin Apostle, who on that account was so dear to his Lord, "the disciple whom Jesus loved," who lay on His bosom, who received His Mother from Him when upon the cross, who had the vision of all the wonders which were to come to pass in the world to the end of time. "Greatly to be honored," says the Church, "is blessed John, who on the Lord's Breast lay at supper, to whom, a virgin, did Christ on the cross commit His Virgin Mother. He was chosen a virgin by the Lord, and was more beloved than the rest. The special prerogative of chastity had made him meet for his Lord's larger love, because being chosen by Him a virgin, a virgin he remained unto the end." He it was who in his youth professed his readiness to drink Christ's chalice with Him, who wore away a long life as a desolate stranger in a foreign land, who was at length carried to Rome, and plunged into the hot oil, and then was banished to a far island until his days drew near their close.

JAMES AND JOHN

Two brothers freely cast their lot
    With David's royal Son;
The cost of conquest counting not,
    They deem the battle won.

Brothers in heart, they hope to gain
    An undivided joy;
That man may one with man remain,
    As boy was one with boy.

Christ heard; and will'd that James should fall,
    First prey of Satan's rage;
John linger out his fellows all,
    And die in bloodless age.

Now they join hands once more above,
    Before the Conqueror's throne;
Thus God grants prayer, but in His love
    Makes times and ways His own.

IT IS THE LORD

For in truth we are not called once only, but many times; all through our life Christ is calling us. He called us first in baptism; but afterwards also; whether we obey His voice or not, He graciously calls us still. . . . He calls us on from grace to grace, and from holiness to holiness, while life is given us. Abraham was called from his home, Peter from his nets, Matthew from his office, Elisha from his farm, Nathanael from his retreat; we are all in course of calling, on and on, from one thing to another, having no resting place, but mounting toward our eternal rest, and obeying one command only to have another put upon us. He calls us again and again, in order to justify us again and again,—and again and again, and more and more, to sanctify and glorify us.

It were well if we understood this; but we are slow to master the great truth, that Christ is, as it were, walking among us, and by His hand, or eye, or voice, bidding us follow Him. We do not understand that His call is a thing which takes place now. We think it took place in the Apostles' days; but we do not believe in it, we do not look out for it in our own case. We have not eyes to see the Lord; far different from the beloved Apostle, who knew Christ even when the rest of the disciples knew Him not. When He stood on the shore after His resurrection, and bade them cast the net into the sea, "that disciple whom Jesus loved saith unto Peter, It is the Lord."

HER UNSEEN LORD

Energetic, direct apprehension of an unseen Lord and Savior has not been peculiar to Prophets and Apostles; it has been the habit of His Holy Church and of her children, down to this day. Age passes after age, and she varies her discipline, and she adds to her devotions, and all with the one purpose of fixing her own and their gaze more fully upon the person of her unseen Lord. She has adoringly surveyed Him, feature by feature, and has paid a separate homage to Him in every one. She has made us honor His Five Wounds, His Precious Blood, and His Sacred Heart. She has bid us meditate on His infancy, and the acts of His ministry; His agony, His scourging, and His crucifixion. She has sent us on a pilgrimage to His birthplace and His sepulcher, and the mount of His ascension. She has sought out and placed before us, the memorials of His life and death; His crib and holy house, His holy tunic, the handkerchief of Saint Veronica, the cross and its nails, His winding-sheet, and the napkin for His head.

And so, again, if the Church has exalted Mary or Joseph, it has been with a view to the glory of His sacred humanity. . . . If we are devout to Joseph, it is as to His foster-father; and if he is the saint of happy death, it is because he died in the hands of Jesus and Mary.

FOSTER-FATHER

Hence at length those luminous stars rose in the ecclesiastical heavens, which were of more august dignity than any which had preceded them, and were late in rising, for the very reason that they were so specially glorious. Those names, I say, which at first sight might have been expected to enter soon into the devotions of the faithful, with better reason might have been looked for at a later date, and actually were late in their coming. Saint Joseph furnishes the most striking instance of this remark; here is the clearest of instances of the distinction between doctrine and devotion. Who, from his prerogatives and the testimony on which they come to us, had a greater claim to receive an early recognition among the faithful than he? A saint of Scripture, the foster-father of our Lord, he was an object of the universal and absolute faith of the Christian world from the first, yet the devotion to him is comparatively of late date. When once it began, men seemed surprised that it had not been thought of before; and now, they hold him next to the Blessed Virgin in their religious affection and veneration.

MERCIFUL

O my dear Lord, have mercy upon me! I trust Thou hast forgiven me my sins—but the punishment remains. In the midst of Thy love for me, and recognizing me as Thine own, Thou wilt consign me to Purgatory. There I shall go through my sins once more, in their punishment. Here is the time for a thorough repentance. Here is the time of good works, of obtaining indulgences, of wiping out the debt in every possible way. Thy saints, though to the eyes of man without sin, really had a vast account— and they settled it by continual trials here. I have neither their merit nor their sufferings. I cannot tell whether I can make such acts of love as will gain me an indulgence of my sins. The prospect before me is dark—I can only rely on Thy infinite compassion. O my dear Lord, who hast in so many ways shown Thy mercy towards me, pity me here! Be merciful in the midst of justice.

FOR EVER

O Emmanuel, O God in our flesh! We too hope, by Thy grace, to follow Thee. We will cling to the skirts of Thy garments, as Thou goest up; for without Thee we cannot ascend. O Emmanuel, what a day of joy when we shall enter heaven! O inexpressible ecstasy, after all trouble! There is none strong but Thou.

ONE VISION

My Lord is gone up into Heaven. I adore Thee, Son of Mary, Jesus Emmanuel, my God and my Savior. I am allowed to adore Thee, my Savior and my own Brother, for Thou art God. I follow Thee in my thoughts, O Thou First Fruits of our race, as I hope one day by Thy grace to follow Thee in my person. To go to heaven is to go to God. . . . Teach me this, O God; give me Thy supernatural grace to practice it; to have my reason, affections, intentions, aims, all penetrated and possessed by the love of Thee, plunged and drowned in the One Vision of Thee.

A Triduo to Saint Joseph
(The Glorious Titles of Saint Joseph)

First Day

He was the true and worthy Spouse of Mary, supplying in a visible manner the place of Mary's Invisible Spouse, the Holy Ghost. He was a virgin, and his virginity was the faithful mirror of the virginity of Mary. He was the Cherub, placed to guard the new terrestrial Paradise from the intrusion of every foe.

V. Blessed be the name of Joseph.
R. Henceforth and for ever. Amen.

Let Us Pray
God, who in Thine ineffable Providence didst vouchsafe to choose Blessed Joseph to be the husband of Thy most holy Mother, grant, we beseech Thee, that we may be made worthy to receive him for our intercessor in heaven, whom on earth we venerate as our holy Protector; who livest and reignest world without end. Amen.

Second Day

His was the title of father of the Son of God, because he was the Spouse of Mary, ever Virgin. He was our Lord's father, because Jesus ever yielded to him the obedience of a son. He was our Lord's father, because to him were entrusted, and by him were faithfully fulfilled the duties of a father, in protecting Him, giving Him a home, sustaining and rearing Him, and providing Him with a trade.

V. Blessed be the name of Joseph.
R. Henceforth and for ever. Amen.

LET US PRAY
God, who in Thine ineffable Providence didst vouchsafe, etc.

THIRD DAY

He is Holy Joseph, because according to the opinion of a great number of doctors, he, as well as Saint John Baptist, was sanctified even before he was born. He is Holy Joseph, because his office, of being spouse and protector of Mary, specially demanded sanctity. He is Holy Joseph, because no other saint but he lived in such and so long intimacy and familiarity with the source of all holiness, Jesus, God incarnate, and Mary, the holiest of creatures.

V. Blessed be the name of Joseph.
R. Henceforth and for ever. Amen.

LET US PRAY
God, who in Thine ineffable Providence didst vouchsafe, etc.

THE MOMENT BEFORE

O what a moment of sympathy between the three, the moment before Joseph died—they supporting and hanging over him, he looking at them and reposing in them with undivided, unreserved, supreme devotion, for he was in the arms of God and the Mother of God. As a flame shoots up and expires, so was the ecstasy of that last moment ineffable, for each knew and thought of the reverse which was to follow on the snapping of that bond. One moment, very different, of joy, not of sorrow, was equal to it in intensity of feeling, that of the birth of Jesus. The birth of Jesus, the death of Joseph, moments of unutterable sweetness, unparalleled in the history of mankind. Saint Joseph went to limbo, to wait his time, out of God's Presence. Jesus had to preach, suffer, and die; Mary to witness His sufferings, and even after He had risen again, to go on living without Him amid the changes of life and the heartlessness of the heathen.

IN PERFECT HARMONY

When, for our sakes, the Son came on earth and took our flesh, yet He would not live without the sympathy of others. For thirty years He lived with Mary and Joseph and thus formed a shadow of the Heavenly Trinity on earth. O the perfection of that sympathy which existed between the three! not a look of one, but the other two understood, as expressed, better than if expressed in a thousand words—nay more than understood, accepted, echoed, corroborated. It was like three instruments absolutely in tune which all vibrate when one vibrates, and vibrate either one and the same note, or in perfect harmony.

ONE HARP WAS SILENT

The first weakening of that unison was when Joseph died. It was no jar in the sound, for to the last moment of his life he was one with them, and the sympathy between the three only became more intense, and more sweet, while it was brought into new circumstances and had a wider range in the months of his declining, his sickness, and death. Then it was like an air ranging through a number of notes performed perfectly and exactly in time and tune by all three. But it ended in a lower note than before, and when Joseph went, a weaker one. Not that Joseph, though so saintly, added much in volume of sound to the other two, but sympathy, by its very meaning, implies number, and, on his death, one, out of three harps, was unstrung and silent.

SAINT MARY MAGDALEN

Wonderful meeting between what was most base and what is most pure! Those wanton hands, those polluted lips, have touched, have kissed the feet of the Eternal and He shrank not from the homage. And as she hung over them, and as she moistened them from her full eyes, how did her love for One so great, yet so gentle, wax vehement within her, lighting up a flame which never was to die from that moment even forever! and what excess did it reach, when He recorded before all men her forgiveness, and the cause of it. "Many sins are forgiven her, for she has loved much; but to whom less is forgiven, the same loveth less. And He said unto her, Thy sins are forgiven thee; thy faith hath made thee safe; go in peace."

Henceforth love was to her as to Saint Augustine and to Saint Ignatius Loyola afterwards (great penitents in their own time), as a wound in the soul so full of desire as to become anguish. She could not live out of the presence of Him in whom her joy lay; her spirit languished after Him, when she saw Him not; and waited on Him silently, reverently, wistfully, when she was in His blissful Presence. We read of her (if it was she), on one occasion, sitting at His feet, and listening to His words; and He testified to her that she had chosen that best part which should not be taken away from her. And, after His resurrection, she by her perseverance, merited to see Him even before the Apostles. She would not leave the Sepulcher, when Peter and John retired, but stood without weeping; and when the Lord appeared to her, and held her eyes that she should not know Him, she said piteously to the supposed keeper of the garden, "Tell me where thou hast laid Him, and I will take Him away." And when at length He made Himself known to her, she turned herself, and rushed to embrace His feet, as at the beginning, but He, as if to prove the dutifulness of her love, forbade her: "Touch Me not," He said, "for I have not yet ascended to My Father; but go to My brethren, and say to them, I ascend to

My Father and your Father, to my God and your God." And so she was left to long for the time when she should see Him, and hear His voice, and enjoy His smile, and be allowed to minister to Him, forever in Heaven.

SAINT PAUL

May this glorious Apostle, this sweetest of inspired writers, this most touching and winning of teachers, may he do me some good turn, who have ever felt a special devotion towards him! May this great saint, this man of large mind, of various sympathies, of affectionate heart, have a kind thought for every one of us here according to our respective needs! He has carried his human thoughts and feelings with him to his throne above; and, though he sees the Infinite and Eternal Essence, he still remembers well that troublous, restless ocean below, of hopes and fears, of impulses and aspirations, of efforts and failures, which is now what it was when he was here.

Let us beg him to intercede for us with the Majesty on High, that we too may have some portion of that tenderness, compassion, and mutual affection, love of brotherhood, abhorrence of strife and division, in which he excelled. . . . that the great name of Paul may be to [us] a tower of strength and fount of consolation now, and in death, and in the day of account.

Zeal and Patience

"I, Paul, the prisoner of the Lord."

O Comrade bold of toil and pain!
    Thy trial how severe,
When sever'd first by prisoner's chain
    From thy loved labor-sphere!

Say, did impatience first impel
    The heaven-sent bond to break?
Or, couldst thou bear its hindrance well,
    Loitering for Jesus's sake?

Oh, might we know! for sore we feel
    The languor of delay,
When sickness lets our fainter zeal
    Or foes block up our way.

Lord! Who thy thousand years dost wait
    To work the thousandth part
Of Thy vast plan, for us create
    With zeal a patient heart.

Saint Monica

Look down then upon us from heaven, O blessed
Monica, for we are engaged in supplying that very
want which called for thy prayers, and gained for
thee thy crown. Thou who didst obtain thy son's
conversion by the merit of thy intercession, continue that intercession for us, that we may be blest,

as human instruments, in the use of those human means by which ordinarily the Holy Cross is raised aloft, and religion commands the world. Gain for us, first, that we may intensely feel that God's grace is all in all, and that we are nothing; next, that, for His greater glory, and for the honor of Holy Church, and for the good of man, we may be "zealous for all the better gifts," and may excel in intellect as we excel in virtue.

SAINT AUGUSTINE

At last he came within the range of a great saint in a foreign country; and, though he pretended not to acknowledge him, his attention was arrested by him, and he could not help coming to sacred places to look at him again and again. He began to watch him and speculate about him, and wondered with himself whether he was happy. He found himself frequently in Church, listening to the holy preacher, and he once asked his advice [on] how to find what he was seeking. And now a final conflict came on him with the flesh: it was hard, very hard, to part with the indulgences of years, it was hard to part and never to meet again. Oh, sin was so sweet, how could he bid it farewell? how could he tear himself away from its embrace, and betake himself to that lonely and dreary way which led heavenwards? but God's grace was sweeter far, and it convinced him while it won him; it convinced his reason, and prevailed; and he who without it would have lived and died a child of Satan, became under its wonder-working power, an oracle of sanctity and truth.

DEUS TUORUM MILITUM

O God, of Thy soldiers
    the Portion and Crown,
Spare sinners who hymn
    the praise of the Blest;
Earth's bitter joys,
    its lures and its frown,
He scann'd them and scorn'd,
    and so is at rest.
The martyr he ran
    all valiantly o'er
A highway of blood
    for the prize Thou hast given.
We kneel at Thy feet,
    and meekly implore,
That our pardon may wait
    on his triumph in heaven.
Honor and praise
    To the Father and Son
    And the Spirit be done
Now and always. Amen.

THE LIGHT IS THE LAMB

For us, my dear Brethren, whose duties lie in a seat of learning and science, may we never be carried away by any undue fondness for any human branch of study, so as to be forgetful that our true wisdom, and nobility, and strength, consist in the knowledge of Almighty God. Nature and man are our studies, but God is higher than all. It is easy to lose Him in His works. It is easy to become over attached in our own pursuit, to substitute it for religion, and to make it the fuel of pride. Our secular attainments will avail us nothing, if they be not subordinate to religion. The knowledge of the sun, moon, and stars, of the earth and its three kingdoms, of the classics or of history, will never bring us to heaven. We may "thank God," that we are not as the illiterate and the dull; and those whom we despise, if they do but know how to ask mercy of Him, know what is very much more to the purpose of getting to heaven, than all our letters and our science. . . . Let us thank Him for all that He has done for us, for what He is doing by us; but let nothing that we know or that we can do, keep us from a personal individual adoption of the great Apostle's words, "Christ Jesus came into this world to save sinners, of whom I am the chief."

INDIVIDUALLY

God has created all things for good; all things for their greatest good; everything for its own good. What is the good of one is not the good of another; what makes one man happy would make another unhappy. God has determined, unless I interfere with His plan, that I should reach that which will be my greatest happiness. He looks on me individually,

He calls me by my name, He knows what I can do, what I can best be, what is my greatest happiness, and He means to give it me.

OUR DAILY TASKS

Did God then send you, above all other men, into the world to be idle in spiritual matters? Is it your mission only to find pleasure in this world, in which we are but as pilgrims and sojourners? Are you more than sons of Adam, who, by the sweat of their brow, are to eat bread till they return to the earth out of which they are taken? Unless you have some work in hand, unless you are struggling, unless you are fighting with yourselves, you are no followers of those who "through many tribulations entered into the kingdom of God." A fight is the very token of a Christian. He is a soldier of Christ; high or low, he is this and nothing else. If you have triumphed over all mortal sin, then you must attack your venial sins; there is no help for it; there is nothing else to do, if you would be soldiers of Jesus Christ. . . .

Everyone is made for his day; he does his work in his day, what he does is not the work of any other day, but of his own day; his work is necessary in order to the work of that next day which is not his, as a stepping-stone on which we, who come next, are to raise our own work. God grant that we too may do our own work, whatever it may be. . . . God in His great mercy grant, by the sacrifice of the Immaculate Lamb, once made on the cross, daily renewed at the altar, through the intercession of His dear Virgin Mother, for the merits of all the saints, especially those connected with this diocese, God, the Holy Trinity, Father, Son, and Holy Ghost, grant us, with unselfish hearts and pure love of Him, ever to aim at His glory, and to seek His will, and to ask for His grace, and to obey His word, laboring according to our strength, laboring to the end—laboring to the very end, in humility, diligence, and love!

YOUR VICTORY

A man finds himself in a definite place; he draws persons around him; they know him, he knows them; thus it is that ideas are born which are to live, that works begin which are to last. . . . Make yourselves and your religion known more and more, for in that knowledge is your victory.

JESUS WITH ME

I know, O my God, I must change, if I am to see Thy face! . . . Body and soul must die to this world. My real self, my soul, must change by a true regeneration. None but the holy can see Thee. . . . Oh, support me, as I proceed in this great, awful, happy change, with the grace of Thy unchangeableness. My unchangeableness here below is perseverance in changing. Let me day by day be molded upon Thee, and be changed from glory to glory, by ever looking towards Thee, and ever leaning on Thy arm. I know, O Lord, I must go through trial, temptation, and much conflict, if I am to come to Thee. I know not what lies before me. I know that if Thou art not with me, my change will be for the worse, not for the better. Whatever fortune I have, be I rich or poor, healthy or sick, with friends or without, all will turn to evil if I am not sustained by the unchangeable; all will turn to good if I have Jesus with me, yesterday and today, the same and for ever.

FOR EACH

Christ's work of mercy has two chief parts; what He did for all men, what He does for each. . . .

They who are living religiously have from time to time truths they did not know before, or had no need to consider, brought before them forcibly; truths which involve duties, which are in fact precepts, and claim obedience. In this and such-like ways Christ calls us now. There is nothing miraculous or extraordinary in His dealings with us. He works through our natural faculties and circumstances of life. Still what happens to us in providence is in all essential respects what His voice was to those whom He addressed when on earth: whether He commands by a visible presence, or by a voice, or by our consciences, it matters not, so that we feel it to be a command. If it is a command, it may be obeyed or disobeyed; it may be accepted as Samuel or Saint Paul accepted it, or put aside after the manner of the young man who had great possessions.

REMEMBER SUCH A ONE

And, O my brethren, O kind and affectionate hearts, O loving friends, should you know anyone whose lot it has been by writing or by word of mouth, in some degree to help you thus to act; if he has ever told you what you know about yourselves, or what you did not know; has ever read to you your wants or feelings, and comforted you by the very reading; has made you feel that there was a higher life than this daily one, and a brighter world than that you see; or encouraged you, or sobered you, or opened a way to the inquiring, or soothed the perplexed; if what he has said or done has ever made you take interest in him, and feel well inclined towards him; remember such a one in time to come, though you hear him not, and pray for him, that in all things he may know God's will, and at all times he may be ready to fulfill it.

AFTERWORD

In his speech on the beatification of Cardinal New-man in the summer of 2010, Pope Benedict XVI noted how much Newman had influenced his own theology over the years. He made it abundantly clear that Newman's blessedness consisted in his living the Christian life to the fullest, such that he can be regarded as an example to and for the Church.

Being a brilliant writer—the nineteenth centu-ry's foremost Christian apologist and the writer of such classics as *A Grammar of Assent* and *Apologia pro Vita Sua*—is not, in and of itself, qualification for blessedness. Newman would agree, having said time and again that accomplishment brings with it the temptation to pride. Nonetheless, Benedict points out that for Newman, there was no divorce between thought and action. Benedict understands well that in the case of Newman, one is dealing, with not sim-ply a theological but a spiritual master, one who laid out the dimensions of Christian life—its basic presuppositions and practices—and who uncovered obstacles to Christian living, obstacles that were embedded in the human condition as well as those that were specifically modern. Newman's beatification—and later canonization—implies the verdict that this particular spiritual master enacted what he spoke about and preached.

This book is a compilation of Newman's spiritual writings by Daniel M. O'Connell, SJ, which precedes Benedict's beatification speech by nearly eighty years (1938). The thematic organization of Newman's writings in this collection—writings penned at various times and for varied occasions—starts with prayers to and reflections on the Holy Trinity. It proceeds through prayers, reflections, and intercessions to Christ, meditations on the Eucharist, reflections on and intercessions to Mary, and culminates in reflections on the saints. O'Connell's arrangement is not simply a matter of tidying up the unruly. It suggests that for Newman, there was no viable form of Christian spirituality that could be segregated from the actual faith of the Church that testifies to the glory of the triune God, the mediatorship of Christ, and the intercessory power of Mary.

Belief, for the Christian, is not something that is "tacked on" to a vague longing for meaning and transcendence so as to give that longing definition and shape. Rather, belief is a kind of pathway to the transcendent reality, a pathway that, for the Christian, is personal—all the way through. For Newman, it is the relationship with the "tri-personal" God that is absolutely defining of who we are as human beings. This relationship shapes our beliefs (and the articulation of those beliefs) as much as it does our more ineffable longings. Newman's basic conviction is that getting this right is the truly essential matter of our lives, relative to which success in all other matters pales. Furthermore, he suggests that however well we would like to think of ourselves, this relationship between us and the triune God is not one of equality.

The magnetic pole of the human being's relation to the divine is the glorious and triune God who is superlatively good and beautiful, as well as true. Reason can provide no true measure as to why this absolutely transcendent and perfect divine being gives so stupendously in creating, redeeming, and sanctifying human beings. For Newman, the only proper way to respond to a God whose being and activity so transcend our capacity to comprehend is to praise and worship. From this flows the practices of prayer and meditation that, in turn, are the ground of specifically Christian action in the world.

The great spiritual writer Louis Bouyer has underscored just how important the stress in Newman is on the object of faith, as throughout his career he elaborated the coordinates of the Christian life. Above all else, there is Newman's fidelity to the tradition of the Church. Newman understood well that throughout history there are various emphases in Christianity, with some Christians tending more nearly to the contemplative, others more nearly to the practical pole; nonetheless, for him there are constants. Although he agrees that these constants impose certain constraints, he is convinced that in the end they prove liberating.

A Christianity that would compromise the transcendence of God by exaggerating the role that we play in making Christianity a true religion is not worthy of the name. Newman is satisfied that the coordinates of faith he supplies are those of the faith of Origen in the third century, Athanasius in the fourth, Augustine in the fifth, Philip Neri in the sixteenth, and Pascal in the seventeenth. No more than in the case of any of these traditional figures does Newman think that the coordinates of faith are purely a theoretical matter. Not knowing who God is, not grasping properly what God has done on our behalf, not only hinders our relationship to him by replacing God with an idol, but misguides us with respect to those practices that allow us to relate to God properly and those forms of life that are vehicles of grace.

The other side to this retrieval of tradition is the apology on behalf of Christianity in general, and Christian life in particular, in and to a world that has grown increasingly secular. As Newman sees it, the forces of secularity have significantly undermined creedal Christianity and done serious damage to the intelligibility and persuasiveness of traditional Christianity's insistence on holiness. Again and again Newman points to the secular caricaturing of Christianity as inhumane and the counterfeits of Christianity that result when Christianity makes a cowardly peace with powers that are inimical to it.

The stripped-down version of Christianity—which is short on the awfulness of the divine, impatient with the characterization of God as triune, skimpy on the presence of God in the world and in the Eucharist, horrified by allotting a role in salvation to Mary—is the point at which all Christianity will arrive unless it recalls the gift of God, focused in the form of the incarnate and crucified Christ. Persuasion can be the individual's task; it is necessarily the task of the Church. But in the end it is a divine accomplishment.

It is appropriate that the last section of this book concerns the saints. Although saints are exceptional, they are not anomalies. The purpose of Christianity is nothing more or less than the making of saints. The saint is the one who is open to God, who discerns and accepts the mission she is given, who understands her sinfulness and frailty and trusts that God can bring about good in and through a frail instrument; but for Newman this is necessarily the description of every Christian. Newman understands from his own experience that only some Christians approximate to the kind of perfection to which all Christians are called. He understands this to be the judgment of the tradition as well. But he does not think that this is an argument against the view that all Christians are called to holiness. Toward this end Newman scrupulously avoids striking any note of spiritual athleticism. A necessary condition of holiness is openness to God's grace, but through-

222 | The Essential Cardinal Newman Collection

out his prayers and meditations, Newman stresses not only the initiative of grace but also its regulating function. He risks the hyperbole: All is grace. The point is that, ultimately, holiness is not a bundle of special qualities but an entire human life that has become transparent to God's goodness, beauty, and truth, and God's saving power in the universe. And it should not come as a surprise that sometimes the saint is made of very crooked timber and reveals idiosyncrasies that hide rather than reveal the holiness of God. This is one reason why there are many kinds of saints as well as many saints.

Holiness, however, consists of more than good intentions; it requires practice to focus the mind on God and his saving work and one's place in God's plan. For Newman, prayer and the liturgy are central. To pray often and well is a Christian mandate: One understands who one is when one prays, that is, a creature before God the creator and sustainer of this magnificent universe, a creature who has been gratuitously redeemed by God in the sacrifice of Christ. When it comes to prayer, Newman has no problem with us asking something of God, although the Christian must ask in the spirit of "thy will be done." But more important than petition is praise. Throughout this book, the emphasis falls conspicuously on praise and thanksgiving rendered to the triune God who is the unstinting giver of gifts, of life, of forgiving and redeeming presence, and of the spirit who makes individuals holy and supports and builds the Church.

Precisely as Christians we are called to pray and to ponder and to do what we can to contribute to the work of sanctification that crucially involves a graced participation in the triune God. As Newman's reflections make clear, many of the challenges to the prospect of a holy life are systemic. There are global, familial, economic, social, and political affairs to which we are obliged to attend. We also have to deal with our tendencies toward distraction, our small-mindedness, our vanity, and above all, our pride. Sin is what damages our relationship with God, who is totally other, and all forms of sin are enclosing forms of self-love in contrast to love of God. Throughout the anthology, with respect to the pairs of sin and redemption and of sin and holiness, Newman comes across as representing the best in the early Church—especially Augustine. But in advocating self-examination, prayer, and sanctioning disciplines such as fasting, Newman also understands himself to be rowing against the current of modern forms of Christianity, which suggest that sin belongs to yesteryear and the imperative of holiness is fanatical and unhealthy. For in the radically "modern" forms of Christianity, the standard proposed for who we should be is the "good enough," the socially adjusted person who will neither pray often nor deeply, who will no more than abide the

Church's liturgy, and who weeds out the over-belief of traditional Christianity.

For Newman, the thinning out of Christianity is quite literally catastrophic, and the religious self that emerges impoverished and flat. This newly minted Christian does not look too carefully in the mirror, while failing entirely to look through the window of the self to adore, praise, and thank God. With this new standard of religiousness in mind, the call to holiness is parodied; the notion of the saint is greeted with incomprehension, and actual saints are ridiculed. This is what is peculiar to the "modern" situation whose identification was one of Newman's foremost tasks throughout his over sixty years of writing.

Forty years after Newman's death in 1890, the compiler of the poems, prayers, and reflections that make up this book understands well that secularity will continue to challenge Christianity and that it would be a mistake for Catholicism to think itself immune. Whatever changes there have been in the subtlety of the secular takeover of Christianity, it can be seen that Newman has powerfully displayed its basic strategies as well as its shape. There is something in Newman's prayers like joyous resistance to it. For Newman, Christianity is the opposite of a creedless religion, and the call to holiness laid out in the creed is not a disposable feature.

At the same time, the call to holiness is not an impossible burden, because holiness is not about self-perfection. Rather, holiness is about being open to God's work; for the person who is in the process of becoming holy, it is God who carries the burden. Moreover, the upshot is a decidedly more tolerant attitude toward failure than that proposed by the advocate of the "good enough." Newman thinks that the personality, which, on the surface of things, embraces the idea of the "good enough," is one that is in fact riddled with anxiety about his or her failure. By contrast, Newman believes that the tradition (and the personality that has interiorized the tradition in her faith) is comfortable with failure precisely because it has a concept of sin and a God who, if a judge, is a truly merciful one! In the last twenty or thirty years, there have been a variety of anthologies that look at Newman's poems, prayers, and reflections. Some stress genre, others chronology. *The Essential Newman Collection* stresses the connection between true faith and right behavior. It still remains an indispensable digest of Newman's thought on the Christian life, and specifically how vision is the root of action. But it also represents something of an extension in that it brings together what was scattered in Newman and suggests ways in which it can be applied to our everyday lives.

Christianity is always about formation. Conversion is marvelous, but it is not enough. Life is a journey in and through which we are continually transformed and conformed to Christ. This requires that our attention be on the triune God and on the discernment of our mission and our call. This requires also that that we continually call to mind what God has done for us. Memory is just as important as attention. But what completes and makes replete the Christian life is the ever renewed sense of gratitude to a God who has shown himself to be love, and who invites me into participation with him.

Cyril O'Regan
Huisking Professor of Theology
University of Notre Dame

SOURCE REFERENCES

Apologia . . . . *Apologia Pro Vita Sua*
Callista . . . . . . Callista: A Tale of the Third Century
D. M. C. . . . . . . Discourses to Mixed Congregations
Dream . . . . Dream of Gerontius
Loss . . . . Loss and Gain
Med . . . . Meditations and Devotions
P. P. S. . . . . Parochial and Plain Sermons
Present . . . Present Position of Catholics in England
S. V. O. . . . . Sermons on Various Occasions
Verses . . . . Verses on Various Occasions
Lectures . . . . Lectures on Justification
S. N. . . . . Sermon Notes
S. S. D. . . . . Sermons on Subjects of the Day

Index of Titles

St. **John Henry Newman** (1801–1890) was an influential Anglican churchman, a dedicated scholar, and a famous British convert to the Catholic Church. After his conversion to Catholicism, he was influential in the founding of the Birmingham Oratory and served as rector of the Catholic University of Ireland. In 1879, he was elevated to the College of Cardinals by Pope Leo XIII.

Newman was canonized on October 13, 2019, by Pope Francis.

Jennifer Newsome Martin is an associate professor in the Program of Liberal Studies and the Department of Theology at the University of Notre Dame.

Cyril O'Regan is the Catherine F. Huisking Professor of Theology at the University of Notre Dame. His primary field of study is systematic theology.

AVE

AVE MARIA PRESS

Founded in 1865, Ave Maria Press,
a ministry of the Congregation of
Holy Cross, is a Catholic publishing
company that serves the spiritual and
formative needs of the Church and its
schools, institutions, and ministers;
Christian individuals and families; and
others seeking spiritual nourishment.

For a complete listing of titles from

Ave Maria Press

Sorin Books

Forest of Peace

Christian Classics

visit www.avemariapress.com

AVE MARIA PRESS
Notre Dame, IN
A Ministry of the United States Province of Holy Cross